THE
EVERYTHING.
Bass Guitar Book

Dear Re   r,

My brot   Nelson and I have worked together as musicians for more
than tw   ty-five years. When the opportunity came up to coauthor a
book,   jumped at the chance to collaborate in a new way.
    Sin   I am a drummer at heart, I recruited Nelson—an award-
winnir   bassist, multi-instrumentalist, and songwriter—to write the
meat   l potatoes of this book. This meant that I worked primarily
on bi   raphical, historical, and theoretical material while Nelson
conc   rated on the essentials of bass instruction.
    V   have tried to make this book user friendly and easy to fol-
low.   have also tried to be as comprehensive and thorough as
pos: e. It's important to realize that one book cannot teach you
eve   ing there is to know about playing an instrument; therefore,
we   e included two appendices in the back of the book designed
to   st you as you continue your musical journey.
             you're a beginner, we hope that *The Everything® Bass Guitar*
Bc   *with CD* will point you in the right direction. If you're already
pl   .ig, we hope this text will serve as a handy and credible resource.
As   ways, rock on!

Welcome to the EVERYTHING Series!

These handy, accessible books give you all you need to tackle a difficult project, gain a new hobby, comprehend a fascinating topic, prepare for an exam, or even brush up on something you learned back in school but have since forgotten.

You can choose to read an *Everything*® book from cover to cover or just pick out the information you want from our four useful boxes: e-questions, e-facts, e-alerts, e-ssentials. We give you everything you need to know on the subject, but throw in a lot of fun stuff along the way, too.

We now have more than 400 *Everything*® books in print, spanning such wide-ranging categories as weddings, pregnancy, cooking, music instruction, foreign language, crafts, pets, New Age, and so much more. When you're done reading them all, you can finally say you know *Everything*®!

QUESTIONS?
Answers to
common questions

FACTS
Important snippets
of information

ALERTS!
Urgent
warnings

ESSENTIALS
Quick
handy tips

DIRECTOR OF INNOVATION Paula Munier

EDITORIAL DIRECTOR Laura M. Daly

EXECUTIVE EDITOR, SERIES BOOKS Brielle K. Matson

ASSOCIATE COPY CHIEF Sheila Zwiebel

ACQUISITIONS EDITOR Lisa Laing

DEVELOPMENT EDITOR Katie McDonough

PRODUCTION EDITOR Casey Ebert

Visit the entire Everything® series at *www.everything.com*

THE
EVERYTHING®
BASS
GUITAR
BOOK
WITH CD

From lines and licks to chords and charts—
all you need to find your groove

Eric Starr and Nelson Starr

avon, massachusetts

*This book is dedicated to our parents, Nelson and Ruth Starr,
who always believed in and encouraged us.*

An Everything® Series Book.
Everything® and everything.com® are registered trademarks of F+W Publications, Inc.

Published by Adams Media, an F+W Publications Company
57 Littlefield Street, Avon, MA 02322 U.S.A.
www.adamsmedia.com

ISBN 10: 1-59869-483-9
ISBN 13: 978-1-59869-483-3

Printed in the United States of America.

J I H G F E D C B A

Library of Congress Cataloging-in-Publication Data
is available from the publisher.

*This book is available at quantity discounts for bulk purchases.
For information, please call 1-800-289-0963.*

Contents

Acknowledgments

We would like to thank Jeffrey Starr for the line art graphics and Marc Schonbrun for the bass neck diagram. Additionally, many thanks to our wives, Patricia and Katherine, for their enduring patience and constant support.

Top Ten Things You'll Learn
from This Book

1. The basics of playing the electric bass guitar including stringing and tuning, holding the bass, picking and plucking, and using an amplifier.

2. How to play rock, pop, blues, jazz, funk, Latin, and other musical styles.

3. The origins and evolution of a variety of musical styles. You'll learn about the history behind the music!

4. Music theory. This book teaches you about music's building blocks. This means scales, chords, rhythms, song structures, and more. You'll also learn how melody and harmony work together.

5. How to read standard notation and bass tablature.

6. How to play well with other members of the rhythm section, including how to groove with the drummer.

7. How to solo or improvise in a variety of styles.

8. How to write unique but practical bass lines.

9. Tips for practicing, which will maximize your efficiency and rate of progress.

10. How to purchase the right bass for you.

Introduction

▶ Welcome to *The Everything® Bass Guitar Book with CD!* This book is designed to teach you how to play the bass guitar. It also teaches you how to think like a musician by developing both your analytical and creative skills. This text will unlock the secrets of music theory, walk you through the basics of playing, teach you how to create bass lines and solos, and instruct you on a variety of musical styles. You will also learn how to set goals, play in a band, motivate yourself, practice efficiently, and much, much more.

The information found in this book is cumulative. That means that you will learn how to play the bass in a methodical, step-by-step fashion. If you're a beginner, it's highly recommended that you read each chapter in numerical order. If you're more experienced, you may target specific material for review or study. Whatever method you choose, it's important to be organized and thoughtful in your approach.

Will you learn everything there is to know about playing the bass from this text? Unfortunately, the answer is no. No publication could ever make such claims. However, you will learn everything you need to get started. Also, if you learn the musical figures contained in each chapter you will develop considerable proficiency in myriad genres and techniques.

As you proceed, this book will encourage you to develop your musical ear, your reading skills (notation), and your understanding of musical styles. It is also hoped that you will feel inspired as you master each new exercise and each new concept. The table of contents reveals the topics covered in this book. However, the text can be broken down into three main categories: how-to guide, biographical and historical information, and resource guide (Appendices A and B). Chapter 1 also serves as a resource guide for those interested in learning about equipment and gear.

The bass guitar is a relatively new instrument. Compared to violins, cellos, trumpets, drums, and many other orchestral instruments, the electric bass guitar is a babe in the woods. Many gifted musicians, entertainers, and inventors have shaped its budding history. In the mid 1930s, Paul Tutmarc created the first electric bass. An inventor from Seattle, Washington, Tutmarc's horizontal electric bass fiddle could be purchased through the Audiovox Manufacturing Company's catalog as early as 1935. Unfortunately, Tutmarc's invention had little impact on music during the Great Depression and World War II. In the postwar years, the six-string electric guitar swept the nation, and the electric bass followed as a practical alternative to the standup bass. American inventor and luthier Leo Fender was the first to mass produce the electric bass. He called it the Fender Precision, and it hit the showrooms of guitar shops in 1951. The Precision, or P-bass, was an innovation in construction (body, neck, fretboard) and electronics (single-coil and humbucking pickups). To this day bassists use the P-bass, although some modifications have been made over the years.

Major contributors to the bass guitar include Paul McCartney, James Jamerson, Jaco Pastorius, and others. As you read through this book be sure to check out information on these innovators. It's important to learn about key players if only to better understand the mechanics of playing the instrument.

Most of all, as you begin your studies, remember that you are now entering into a kind of musical brotherhood or fellowship. You will also be contributing to the great conversation of music. Because of this, you have a responsibility to be thoughtful and diligent in all you do. So keep an open mind, practice hard, and listen to the expert musicians who have come before you. If you do this, you will earn the right to call yourself a bass player.

Chapter 1

Getting the Right Equipment

Buying the right gear is an important first step toward becoming a bassist. In this opening chapter, you will learn the dos and don'ts of buying and caring for a bass. Additionally, you will learn about amplifiers and other accessories such as guitar stands, cases, cables, effects pedals, and more. Most importantly, this chapter will show you how to choose equipment to meet your individual needs.

Buying an Electric Bass

When it comes to buying an electric bass the options can seem overwhelming. However, the good news is that you can now find quality instruments, at a fair price, at chain stores, mom-and-pop shops, and online. Many beginner and intermediate-level basses are made in China, Korea, and Mexico, and some of these are sold at incredibly low prices. If you're contemplating buying an instrument it's perfectly acceptable to consider these cheaper alternatives; but remember, you often get what you pay for in terms of sheer quality, craftsmanship, and tone.

You might also consider used equipment. In fact, a used instrument may prove to be the best overall value. But just as some people prefer to decorate their home with antiques and some prefer brand-new furnishings, the decision between purchasing a new or used instrument can come down to personal taste. Nevertheless, there are some basic considerations to examine when purchasing a bass.

Before you can make your dream purchase a reality, you must first assess how much money you are willing to invest. First, think about your musical needs. There is no real sense in buying the absolutely finest instrument, which will cost proportionately more, if you are a beginner.

For more intermediate players, bass prices can really vary. You might be looking at anywhere between $300 and $1,000, depending on the specific features that you seek. For the advanced player, it is not unusual to spend over $1,000 for a high-end electric bass. At all purchase levels, you will have to decide what level of personal commitment you are willing to make as a musician. You need to think about what features in a bass you really want and, most importantly, what features you really need.

The Right Fit

There are so many types and styles of electric basses that it may seem as if picking one is like choosing your favorite flavor of ice cream at an ice cream parlor. Thankfully, the task of choosing a bass is a lot more practical and rational than that. Often, the best choice comes down to picking the right tool for the job. In short, your instrument should reflect the type of music you are playing.

Think about what kind of music you want to play, and then research what instruments artists in that genre tend to use. If it's a famous bass player, you can often find this information online or in magazines. You'll find that there is a connection between brand names, models, and musical styles.

For example, if your intention is to perform traditional country music in a band setting, a more traditional electric bass, whose style is reminiscent of basses produced in the 1950s and 1960s, might be a suitable choice. On the other hand, if you are looking to play R & B, you might opt for a modern bass, one that gives you extra slap and punch so that you can sound funky.

Other issues that you should consider have to do with the exact features and details of each electric bass. These include specifications for wood, electronics, size and scale, neck and body contours, general tone, and, again, cost. A more recent development concerning the electric bass is the addition of supplemental strings. Five- and six-string models are now commonplace. These additional strings increase the range of the instrument, but unless you have a specific need or desire to utilize these extended low and high ranges, it won't be necessary to purchase a five- or six-string bass.

Don't forget to check out manufacturers' Web sites. There you will find lots of technical information about basses. For example, Gibson's Web site (*www.gibsonbass.com*) offers information about bodies, necks, fingerboards, hardware, electronics, strings, and cases.

As for the color, that is one of the most personal and subjective choices a purchaser can make. Different colors and finishes are constantly being employed. Due to the vastly expanding terrain of finishing techniques, it is more important than ever to check with your dealer and manufacturer regarding proper care. Choose a finish that suits your personal tastes and the genre that you intend to perform. Above all else, before purchasing an instrument, don't be afraid to ask the seller detailed questions. Also, if you're purchasing a bass through a retailer, be sure to ask the sales clerk about the terms and conditions of the sale including return policies and warranties.

Buying an Amplifier

The relationship between the bass guitar and an amplifier is vital. After all, you won't be able to produce the specific sound you desire if you have the wrong amp. The amp is what brings the electric bass to life. Furthermore, the amp has the ability to modify the sound of the bass by changing its tone, volume, and, in some cases, adding distortion, reverb, or other effects. Like basses, the purchase of an amplifier must reflect the buyer's needs. In addition to budget restrictions, musical needs must be considered too. For example, if you plan to play in a loud rock band, you will need an amp that, at the very least, can be turned up loudly. On the other hand, if you plan to accompany a pianist at church services, then a softer, smaller amplifier will do just fine.

There is a wide range of amps available to you at different price points. Buying a used amp is certainly worth considering. However, as is the case with most electronics purchases, you have to make sure that the unit is truly in good working order as most purchases on used amps come without any type of warranty.

There are basically two types of bass amps: combos (where both the speaker and the electronics portions of the amp are housed in the same, single enclosure) and bass amps featuring a speaker cabinet and amp "head" (in separate enclosures). Often, a combo bass amp is smaller to mid-sized, easier to cart around, and proportionately less loud. Bass amps that feature separate enclosures for the speaker cabinet and amp head are often for the professional bassist or for someone who needs to play very loud. The cabinet and head portions are commonly sold separately and are a more "boutique" setup; they offer the bassist a more creative approach to assembling his "dream" bass amp.

Some of the features you will want to consider when making your amp purchases include:

- **The dimensions of the cabinet and speaker itself.** Generally speaking, the louder you wish to play, the larger these need to be.
- **How you'll transport the amp.** If you have a spacious car or van, a large, heavy cabinet may not be hard to schlep. However, if you own a compact car or regularly take mass transit, you will want to look into smaller, more portable options.
- **The tone knobs and other dials.** These items add variability to your sound.
- **Tubes versus solid-state.** Tube amps offer a warmer, vintage sound. Solid-state amps generally offer a cleaner sound.
- **The wattage of the amp.** Wattage is another indicator of the unit's loudness.

Other Accessories

There are some other essential products that you will need to buy before you can get started. First and foremost, you need a guitar cable (sometimes referred to as a guitar cord). The cable is what connects the electric bass to the amplifier. Simply connect the two male ends of the guitar cable to the female inputs on the bass guitar and amplifier.

Unless you want to get real fancy, the type of cable that is needed for an electric bass is the same as the one you would use for an electric guitar or keyboard. The dimensions at the end, or tip, of the cable (referred to as the *jack*) are ¼ inch. Sometimes the cable is also referred to as a *quarter-inch jack*. These cables are readily available at any music store for anywhere from $5 to $50 (and up) depending on the quality. Unless you are recording electric bass for a really high-end project, you can probably make do with a relatively cheap but well-made cable.

You will also need to purchase strings and a strap. When you purchase your electric bass, it should come with strings already on it. If it is a brand new instrument, the strings may or may not be new or fresh. New strings tend to sound brighter and more alive, whereas older ones may sound dull and muted. Apart from the sound, one indication of old strings is that they may be lacking the shiny metallic look that fresh strings have. This may be due to corrosion or debris deposited on the strings from people playing or testing out the bass. If this is the case, then you may want to consider restringing the bass with a fresh set of strings (see Chapter 2). Also, because strings can break from time to time, you might want to purchase a backup set from which to replace a single string should it break.

FACT

There are many different manufacturers and manufacturing processes that can result in different types of strings. Each process produces a unique sound based upon the thickness of the string, the amount and kinds of windings that are applied, and the metals that make up the wire.

Strings can cost anywhere from $5 to $30 and up depending on issues such as metal composition and machine versus hand winding. The thickness of the string is referred to as the *gauge* of the string. For electric basses, these gauges can range from rather thick, or heavy-gauge, strings to medium- or light-gauge strings. Generally, the heavier the string the more solid is the sound. Heavier strings also tend to hold pitch better when struck and don't waiver as much over the course of a note's sustain. Lighter strings, although easier on the fingers and hands, tend to hold pitch more tenuously. Lighter gauges can have a snappier sound that may be better for certain types of music. Again, it all depends on what kind of ensemble and genre you intend to perform in or what sound suits your particular vision.

One common choice when purchasing strings is the decision to go with *round-wound* or *flat-wound* strings. The most popular choice is the round-wound string, which gets its name from the fact that the windings that are wrapped around the core of the string are round in shape. Round-wounds tend to have a brighter, more metallic sound when struck. An alternative is the flat-wound string that, as you might imagine, is wound with a flat winding. These strings have a more muted, less bright sound that somewhat mimics an upright acoustic bass. Because of this, the flat-wound sound may be optimal in styles such as bluegrass and straight-ahead jazz.

As for a strap, this is a very personal choice in which your sense of individual style can really come into play. As long as the strap can be adjusted to a length that suits your body size, the style is up to you. Leather is a common material that is used to manufacture straps, but synthetics are also popular and can be less expensive.

Electronic Accessories and Effects

As you will learn in Chapter 2, tuning refers to the tensioning of the strings to specific pitches. Probably the most highly regarded accessory you can invest in, although optional, is an electronic tuner. Often battery powered, these relatively inexpensive devices can save a player, especially a beginner, from serious frustration.

Tuning a bass is never easy. Due to the low frequency content of a bass's sound, it can be very difficult to hear or to discern the exact pitch of a bass. Luckily for the electric bass player, you can plug it into the tuner, read the meter, and match up the pitch of the string to be exactly in tune. Make sure to choose a tuner that is suited for the electric *bass*—some only work for the higher-pitched electric guitar!

FACT

Pitch is the frequency of a note, which is measured in cycles per second. In the modern era, concert A—located a major sixth above middle C— is set at 440 hertz (Hz). This is the standard pitch that orchestras tune their instruments to.

Effects, whether they are pedals or more elaborate outboard gear, make up the least crucial aspect of what you may need to get started. Often, a bass player may not need any at all. The sound of a well-made and maintained electric bass played through a good-quality amp is often all you really need. Nevertheless, some players, with justification, prefer to augment this basic sound with effects.

Effects can range widely in how they may modify or change your sound. Probably the most popular effect for electric bass is a compressor. Whether purchased in pedal form or as a rackmountable module, this effect reduces the dynamic peaks of a performance and can help the bass find a better fit within the ensemble. An equalizer is also a fairly common addition. Also known as an *EQ*, equalizer units can help sculpt the particular tone you desire by boosting or cutting certain tonal frequencies. Delay, modulation, and reverb effects are less common on the bass but have been known to be employed to very creative ends. Effects are an extension of your creativity and can help expand and broaden your artistic possibilities.

Equipment Maintenance

With the substantial investment you've made in securing your electric bass, amp, and other accessories, it makes sense to think about maintenance. To prolong the life of your musical possessions, there are some simple steps you can take that will dramatically affect longevity.

It's reasonable to expect that, with proper care, your electric bass will last for a lifetime. One way to prolong the lifespan of your instrument is to regularly use a bass case and a bass stand. Often taken for granted, these two rather ubiquitous items add up to an enormous amount of protection and are the first line of defense against unintended accidents.

The first item, the case, is what will prove most crucial. Generally, the sturdier the case, the better, especially if you will be going out and playing live gigs. If you end up on tour, a highly reinforced road case is a must. But even a gig bag, which is a soft-shell padded case, can offer a good deal of protection.

Storage is also crucial to bass maintenance. Always store your bass in a dry, cool place. Never keep your bass near a radiator or other heat source, as this can warp the wood and weaken the glue that may hold the bridge or other important parts in place.

The guitar stand (often the same for basses and guitars) is a great investment. Usually available for well under $50 dollars, a sturdy stand will prevent your electric bass from taking a nasty spill. Because of their long necks and bad center of gravity, electric basses are even more prone to tipping over than electric guitars. So make sure that your bass is always in a secure stand once it is out of the case.

What's a Setup?

Every six months to a year you should have your electric bass examined and set up by an experienced technician or luthier. A luthier is a highly trained and certified guitar builder and repair technician. During this process, the technician will adjust the neck, bridge, and other aspects of the tuning mechanism as well as inspect the electronics and all other aspects of the instrument's health. Often the technician will apply a fresh set of strings and a good polish to the instrument. Make sure to specifically ask the technician to inspect all aspects of the instrument's health and to suggest any repairs or procedures that may be needed.

Finally, there are some small, additional things you can do to keep your instrument in good shape. Keeping your bass in tune as much as possible is always a good idea. This is the optimal tension that the bass has been designed to keep. So it is natural that this will keep the instrument within a zone of comfort by reducing the amount of play that the bass will have to endure. Also, it is a good idea to change the strings regularly (about every one to six months, depending on amount of use) and to polish the fretboard and entire body of the instrument with a guitar polishing cloth and guitar or neck polishing solution. As always, check the manufacturer's recommendations as far as types of polish and cloth.

The Amp and Accessories

The amplifier is a highly complex piece of electrical gear that should never be serviced or manipulated electronically except by a trained and licensed professional. Tube amps in particular have potentially fatal voltage levels, even when the amp is turned off. It is often common to have to send the unit back to the actual manufacturer to be repaired or serviced. If you have a problem or breakdown with your amp, be sure to have it serviced by someone who has been authorized by the manufacturer of that specific brand name or make of amplifier; otherwise, the warranty may become void.

If you own an amplifier that uses vacuum tubes, you may have to have them replaced when they become degraded. Only an authorized repair technician can say for sure when or if that is the case. Unintentional feedback or other audible anomalies may be an indication that the tubes require replacement.

Besides keeping the exterior laminate or wood enclosure of the amp clean (as you would furniture or your car's vinyl interior), there is not much you need to do besides keeping the amp dry and unexposed to extreme temperatures. When it comes to accessories such as effects pedals, you should not attempt to manipulate them beyond replacing the batteries. As for cabling, make sure to wind up your chord after each use. This helps to prolong the life of the cable.

Chapter 2
Getting Started

It's time to pick up your bass and begin playing. In this chapter, you will learn about the key components of the bass including its three "systems." You will also learn how to hold and position the bass. Plus, this chapter includes tips on right- and left-hand finger movement. Lastly, you will learn how to string and tune a bass plus properly use an amplifier.

The Anatomy of the Electric Bass

The electric bass is essentially comprised of a body, a neck, a headstock, a tailpiece, and electronics. It's important to know the names of these individual parts because each component contributes to the bass's overall sound. Every bass is different; however, three basic systems can be organized out of the individual components:

1. Neck and body system
2. Tuning system
3. Electronic system

See **FIGURE 2–1** for a comprehensive list of the most important parts on the bass. Included in this pictorial are components of all three systems.

FIGURE 2–1.
The anatomy
of the bass

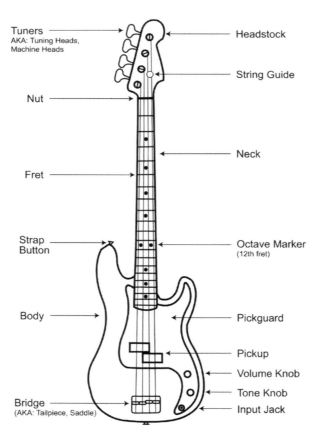

Tuners
AKA: Tuning Heads,
Machine Heads

Headstock

String Guide

Nut

Neck

Fret

Strap
Button

Octave Marker
(12th fret)

Body

Pickguard

Pickup

Volume Knob

Tone Knob

Bridge
(AKA: Tailpiece, Saddle)

Input Jack

The neck and body system contribute to the overall aesthetic of the instrument. The shape, weight, and materials that comprise this system also influence its natural or unamplified tone. Since the components that comprise this system are primarily manufactured from carved wood, body and neck contours vary from company to company and model to model.

The second system deals with tuning. From the tuning mechanism on the headstock to the bridge and tailpiece, these components make it possible for the strings of the bass to change pitch and hold its tune. Additionally, the nut, truss rod (not shown), and machine heads contribute to the tuning of the instrument (**SEE FIGURE 2–1**).

Lastly, the electric system is defined by windings around a magnet and an electrical current that is outputted to an amplifier. The components that transduce, conduct, and, attenuate this signal are the basis for the electrical system. The pickups (essentially electromagnets—magnets wrapped by coils of wire) capture the initial sound as electrical energy. This energy is then transferred through wires to volume potentiometers and tone controls. In the last stage, this energy is sent to the output jack and sent through the guitar cable to your amp. Toggle switches determine which pickups or combinations of them are employed (although many bass guitars do not have toggle switches). Different types of pickups, together with toggle switch positions and the tone knob, determine the overall tonal quality.

Taking Your First Steps

If you're just starting out, you need to know some very basic information about positioning the bass. The first step is learning how to hold the instrument. Start out in a sitting position. Place the body of the bass so that it rests with the bottom cutaway on your right thigh. When you do this, the bass neck will point to your left. Next, balance the instrument by tilting the neck slightly upward. Finally, place your right forearm over the rear hump on the top edge of the instrument's body.

Use the natural weight of your right arm to help balance the bass in a more secure hold between your right forearm and your right thigh. When in place, bring your left arm up underneath the neck. Place your left thumb on the backside of the neck and, while rounding out your left hand (as if holding a lemon), place your fingertips on the strings. In the right hand, place your index finger on any of the strings. You are now in position to play the bass. If you wish to try standing instead of sitting, keep every position instruction the same except: let the strap, and gravity itself, hold the bass in position against your body while the right forearm is freed up. This is illustrated in **FIGURE 2–2**.

FIGURE 2–2.

Holding the bass

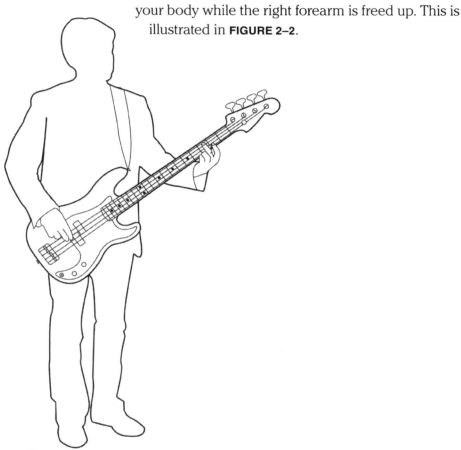

If you plan to play bass right-handed, follow the instructions in this section verbatim. If you are going to play lefty, simply switch around the directions to make right left and left right. Most people play right-handed, but if you feel more comfortable playing lefty go for it.

Plucking or Picking the Strings

As you are holding your bass, the strings are labeled from top to bottom, or from closest to you to furthest away, E, A, D, and G. Take your right index finger and place its tip on any string except the thickest one, which is the E string. Though it may seem unnatural, extend the finger fully straight then press the string toward the body of the bass. Don't actually pluck the bass, just let the tension of the string release and slip out from under your fingertip. When this occurs, your finger should recoil off the string and land on the adjacent string one string level up (toward your face). For example, if you release the G string, the string furthest away from you, your finger will land on the D string. If you release the D string, your finger will land on the A string. And if you release the A string, your finger will land on the E string. Practice this technique using your index and middle fingers. The more you do it, the more comfortable and natural it will become (**SEE FIGURE 2–3**).

FIGURE 2–3.
Right-hand
position

Using a pick, or plectrum, is also an option. A pick works better for some styles of music such as heavy metal or punk. On the other hand, finger playing is usually expected for jazz, country, and R & B. To use a pick, simply hold the pick between your right thumb and index finger so that the point of the pick points toward the bass and away from your thumb at a right angle. Drive the pick down through the intended string then let it come to rest on the next adjacent string. When you do this, it should mute the adjacent string only. Next, reverse the picking to an upward motion. Combine the downward and upward motions to create fluid rhythms. You can become quite fast at picking by combining the down and up techniques into one connected, back-and-forth motion.

Playing an electric bass is a little bit like using a bow. In archery, you draw the bowstring back then release the tension. This drives the arrow. You don't pluck the bow; you simply draw it back and let it snap forward. The same is true on a bass guitar.

To further refine your left-hand movement on the neck of the bass, you may have to do some stretching of your fingers. Start off by placing each finger consecutively on frets one through four on the G string. The G string is highest in pitch and furthest away from your face. Fret one is nearest to the nut; fret two is one fret further from the nut, and so on. Your fingers should be numbered in the same exact fashion so that finger one (index finger) should be on fret one, finger two (middle finger) should be on fret two, and so on.

Keep your left hand and fingers rounded (as if holding a lemon) while pressing the string against the fretboard. Next, add finger movement (or picking) in the right hand. Once you do this, you're up and running.

FIGURE 2–4.
Left-hand
position

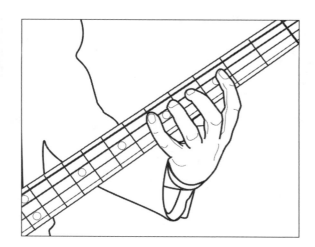

For now, don't be concerned about the bass being out of tune. Also, don't worry about the tone. Just get used to using both hands on the instrument. When depressing the string in the left hand, the position for this is in between the metal frets, toward the front of the rightmost fret (see **FIGURE 2–4**).

Stringing a Bass

Regardless of the brand or type of string you choose, the technique for stringing the bass is essentially the same. First, remove the old string(s) from the instrument by rotating the tuners in whatever direction slackens the string. Next, remove the string from the tuning peg and slide it out from behind the tailpiece (repeat for additional strings). You may dispose of the string at this time. Also, this is a good time to polish the neck of the bass, since there are no strings there to get in your way!

Next, unravel the first string to be applied. The order of stringing is up to you. First, slide the tip of the string (the part without the attached anchoring piece, called the *ball*) into the tailpiece hole. Glide the string, carefully, through the tailpiece and up to the tuning peg. Make sure the end of the string with the ball is now snug in the tailpiece socket. Insert the string tip end through the channel or hole in the tuning peg while still leaving enough slack for the string to be wrapped around the peg after winding about three times.

On most basses, the tuning mechanism is found on the headstock of the instrument. To raise the pitch or tighten a string, you will turn the tuning key in a counterclockwise direction. Some basses (like the headless Steinberger) contain a tuning mechanism on the body of the bass. In this case, you will tighten a string by turning the tuning key in a clockwise direction. Just use common sense and listen to the pitch either rising or lowering.

Most bass guitar tuning pegs use a channel rather than a discrete hole. It is often best to manually tuck the string into the channel, give it one rotation around (by hand), and then secure the string tip in the center hole of the channel. This sets the string. After this procedure, rotate the tuner (also called a machine head) so that the slack is drawn up and wound around the peg. Always wind the string in neat rows around the peg. This ensures that any slack will be removed. It will also prevent any slippage. As you might guess, slippage undermines intonation of the bass.

Finally, make sure that as you tighten the string it is further guided into proper placement over the bridge saddle and threaded through the correct groove in the nut. In order to make sure that this turns out well, be patient and orderly in your procedure. Neatness counts. Proper stringing means better intonation. It also means less unexpected string breaks.

Tuning a Bass

There are many ways to go about tuning your bass, some easier and more accurate than others. What matters most is that your bass is in tune before you play. When people speak of tuning they are referring to the pitch of the instrument. *Pitch* is the perceived frequency of a sound. Standard pitch is A4, or 440 Hz. This means that musicians all agree that the A note above middle C will be equivalent to 440 cycles per second. A4 acts as a kind of center or home base, a point of reference for other pitches.

FACT

A cycle is one complete revolution or wavelength of sound. Thus, an A above middle C makes 440 complete revolutions in one second. The higher the pitch the more cycles per second, while the lower the pitch the less cycles per second.

Tuning with an Electronic Tuner

The easiest way to tune your bass is to use an electronic tuner. Electronic tuners have come down in price so dramatically that virtually anyone can afford one. There are, however, variations in quality between some cheaper units and more pricey ones. Generally, the extremely inexpensive tuners are less reliable and may only be able to tune to standard settings

(E, A, D, G). In other words, if you use a five-string bass or alternate tunings, inexpensive tuners may not be as useful.

Nevertheless, for the most part electric tuners are invaluable. It's difficult to tune an electric bass. This is especially true in live settings where the room and crowd may be too loud to hear the delicate nuances needed to get the pitch just right. Furthermore, performers may need to re-tune on stage in the heat of the moment. When playing at extremely loud volumes, this is difficult to do without an electric tuner.

To use a tuner, all that is needed is a nine-volt battery and a guitar cable. Simply turn the unit on, plug the bass into the tuner, and make sure your bass's volume and tone knobs are fully forward. Next, check the pitch of the individual strings against the pitches that you would like to tune to. The standard tuning of a bass is, from the low to the high, E, A, D, and G. No matter what string you tune, the meter on the unit should stay roughly at the center point throughout the duration of the note's sustain. When it does, the string is in tune. It's really that easy!

Make sure that the indicator lights on the electronic tuner signal that you are actually tuning to the specific note that you desire to. It can be all too easy to tune perfectly to the wrong note. Also, make sure that your pitch is in the ballpark to begin with. If you are way off, you should tune roughly by ear first so that you don't "confuse" the tuner.

Through the use of electronic tuners, a lot of unnecessary stress can be removed from the equation. Since music can be stressful, especially in live situations, it is comforting to know that there is a device out there that can help ease that tension.

Tuning by Ear

Although tuning with an electronic tuner is now commonplace, the art and practical necessity of being able to tune by ear is still something not to be neglected by any musician. Tuning by ear will help to develop your overall sense of pitch. There may also be times where you want to make music and you, for whatever reason, don't have a tuner. Also, tuners sometimes break or batteries run out. Occasionally this happens five minutes before show time! You never know when you may need to fall back on just your ear for tuning.

There is one basic procedure for tuning by ear and two common methods to help realize it. Unless you have perfect pitch, you always need a reference pitch. Any source, including pitch pipes, pianos, keyboards, or guitars, may do. All that really matters is that the reference pitch is as close to perfection as is possible. This means that you can hear the fundamental pitch well.

When tuning by ear, first you must choose a specific reference pitch from the musical alphabet. Although any note can work, for now start with E. Since this pitch is low, you may want to use an amp in order to hear it clearly. Listen carefully to the highness or lowness of the reference pitch, then turn the tuning key higher or lower accordingly. Make sure that the two pitches match before you move on. Once you are confident that the two pitches are the same, use the E string as your new point of reference.

Depress the E string at the fifth fret (counting away from the headstock). When you do this, the note that sounds will be an A. Next, pluck the A string. If it is out of tune, turn the A string's tuning key up or down until it matches the A performed on the E string. Repeat this operation with the remaining two higher-pitched strings until all of them are in tune with each other and the original reference pitch. In other words, press the fifth fret of the A string so that you get a D, then press the fifth fret of the D string so that you get a G. This is a common method used to tune both basses and guitars.

If the pitch is lower than it is supposed to be, it is *flat*. If the pitch is higher than it is supposed to be, it is *sharp*. Strings often go flat during use as they stretch or as slippage occurs.

The second, more complex, way to tune the bass from an initial reference pitch is to use harmonics. This is one of the best methods for tuning an electric bass. However, harmonic tuning is much more complex so beginners shouldn't worry about it just yet. In any case, you must first learn about harmonics, including how to play them. For more information on harmonics see Chapter 8.

Putting Together Your Setup

Now that you have the necessary tools at hand and you've experimented with some playing, it's time to set up your bass rig. First, you should attach the strap to the bass. You may have to adjust the length of the strap so that it doesn't hang too low or high. Make sure that the holes on the strap are secured fully over the strap buttons at both ends of the bass guitar body.

Once your bass is in tune, connect the cables and plugs. Then find an AC outlet so that you can plug the amplifier in. Once you're plugged in, if your amp has a standby switch, engage it so that it has a softer startup. Also, turn the volume controls all the way down. Be careful: there may be multiple volume knobs, or attenuators. Now you are ready to turn the amp on. After switching the amp's power on, give it a few moments to warm up. In the meantime, insert one end of the guitar cable into the jack of the electric bass, then insert the other end into the first jack (sometimes the only jack) on the left side of the amp.

ALERT!

Be sure to always consult the owner's manual before using any electrical device. Overall, tubes are more finicky than transistors. Consequently, tube amps should be turned to standby for at least one minute before use. After use, turn your tube amp to standby again until the tubes cool.

At this point, if the amp has a standby switch, bring it out of standby. Turn the bass guitar's volume knob up slightly—about halfway. Next, slowly turn up the master volume knob on the amplifier. You may or may not hear anything by now. Play a note, any note. If there is no sound yet, you may have to turn up the preamp gain knob or the other volume knob(s) as well as the master volume. If you only have one volume knob and there is no sound, turn up the volume knob on the electric bass and amp until there is sound. Eventually, with some experimentation, you should be able to achieve a basic amplified sound. Now, make some noise!

Chapter 3
Notation and Tablature

In this chapter you will learn about standard notation. You will also learn about tablature, a user-friendly system of notation used for guitar and bass music. In order to use this book effectively, you will need to understand both styles of notation. All of the musical examples found herein use notes and rests, tablature, or a combination of the two. So if you're fuzzy about reading music, don't skip this tutorial.

Notation Overview

Reading music is very important. You should learn how to read music for the same reasons you learn how to read words. If you're musically literate, your chances of survival in the world of music are greatly improved. Musical notation is also an important educational tool. Through notation you will be able to visualize bass parts better and be able to conceive of music more clearly.

This is not to say that playing by ear is wrong or bad. Listening cannot be underestimated, and all musicians should learn how to pick up a tune by ear. However, playing only by ear is limiting, especially when you are trying to learn information from a book. The CD in the back of this guide is a great supplement, but it cannot replace the notation found in each chapter. Therefore, in order to get the most out of this text, make sure you learn how to read music.

All music can be divided into two parts: sound and silence. Notes represent the sounds a musician makes. Rests indicate silence. Both are written on a staff. A staff is a set of five parallel lines on which a composer writes notes, rests, and other musical symbols. **FIGURE 3–1** shows a blank staff.

FIGURE 3–1.
A blank staff

The lines and spaces on a staff represent pitch varieties, and a clef is used to name each line and space. The most common clefs are treble or G clef and bass or F clef. As a bass player, you will only use the bass clef.

Bass Clef

The bass clef is used to represent notes in the lower pitch range of music. When reading or writing music for the bass guitar, the bass clef and staff are used exclusively. Because the bass is so low in pitch, the notes that appear on the bass clef are written one octave higher than the true pitch of the instrument. This is done to keep the bulk of the written notes centered on the staff itself and not consistently below it. However, this means that the bass will sound one octave lower than the written notes. Fortunately, this issue may only become relevant if you need to communicate specific pitches to other musicians.

An *octave* is eight steps above or below any given pitch. Steps are measured as intervals. An *interval* is the space or distance between two notes. An octave always shares the same letter name as its source note, for example, A and A, or C and C. An octave is also one half or double the frequency of its original source pitch.

No matter what clef you're using, musical notes follow the alphabet in the order A–G. After G, the notes repeat again starting with A. Collectively, these notes are called *naturals*. Reading the bass clef is, in principle, the same as reading the treble clef except that the alphabetical note values are shifted down one line or space position. For example, a C is found one space lower on the bass clef than on the treble clef. Moreover, it sounds three octaves lower on a bass. This is shown in **FIGURE 3–2**.

FIGURE 3–2.
Comparing clefs

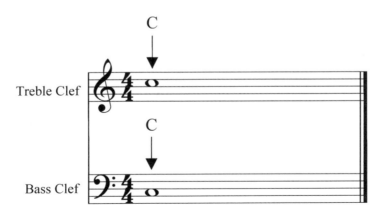

On a piano, these notes would be two octaves apart.
On a bass, the bottom C sounds three octaves lower.

Once the F line has been established, it is relatively easy to find the other notes on the bass clef by moving up or down the staff. For example, since line four (from the bottom) is F, the space above it must be G (one letter higher). Moving in the other direction, if line four is F, then one space below line four must be E.

QUESTION?

What is an F clef?
An F clef is the same as a bass clef. If you imagine a lowercase F turned backwards, you will see the true symbolic origins of the bass clef. In order to find F on the bass clef staff, simply find the line that straddles the clef's two dots.

An easy way to remember the spaces of the bass clef is to use the mnemonic *All Cows Eat Grass* (A, C, E, and G). To remember the lines of the staff use *Good Boys Do Fine Always* (G, B, D, F, and A). This is illustrated in **FIGURE 3–3**.

FIGURE 3–3. Bass clef and pitches

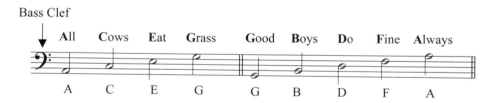

The Range of the Bass

The bass's common range on the staff extends from the lowest note, open E, which is one line below the five-line bass staff (lines written above or below the staff are called *ledger* lines), all the way to D-sharp (on the twentieth fret of the bass), which is so high that it needs octave signs (8va) to designate it. Most written bass music is either on the staff or slightly above or below it. In some cases, it is extended through the use of ledger lines or octave signs to achieve pitches in the higher range of the instrument.

Adding strings to the electric bass increases its range. It is most common to add an additional lower string that extends the low end of the bass all the way to B. This would necessitate the addition of one ledger line with the low B on the space below that ledger line. If a high string is added, it is usually a C. This extends the bass so high that bass clef notation becomes almost silly at the higher extremities.

When it comes to notation, one issue that plagues all multiple-string instruments is their extended range. Further complicating the matter is that each string's range overlaps the other's to one extent or another. This means that a single note may be achieved by playing it on any number of strings. For example, a G written on the fourth space of the bass staff may be played either on the open G string, the fifth fret of the D string, the tenth fret of the A string, or the fifteenth fret of the E string. Although regular notation is best at describing pitch and rhythm, it has no means of indicating the best or proper position on the neck to play a given passage of music, hence the use of tablature.

Understanding Tablature

Often referred to as *tab*, tablature is a system of notation used for fretted string instruments such as guitar and electric bass. Tab is a relatively easy way to communicate the intricacies of neck positioning and note selection. Because there are so many options regarding where to play a note on the bass guitar, a notation system such as tab can help solve this dilemma.

FACT

In Europe, the use of tablature dates back to the fourteenth century. Initially, tab was used as a system of notation for lutes and other plucked instruments such as the orbo, mandora, and vihuela. France, Italy, and Germany all offered variations in tablature notation.

theorbo

Tab tells you the precise order of the notes and the exact string and fret to play them on. For the modern bassist, tab is most commonly used to figure out a bass line from a favorite recording. It also may be used to communicate the best path on the fretboard for any given song or passage.

On bass, tab is arranged on the page as four horizontal lines with numbers written on those lines. The lines represent the four strings of the electric bass with the lowest pitched string—the E string—as the lowest line and the highest pitched string—the G string—as the highest line. The middle two lines represent the middle A and D strings. The numbers, which sit directly on these string lines, indicate the fret numbers on each string that should be depressed.

For example, if you see a "4" on the lowest or E-string line, that means that you will be playing the fourth fret, which is a G-sharp or A-flat. An "o" placed on a line tells you to play an open or unfretted string. Always read the numbers left to right and take note of the spacing; the spacing determines the basic timing of the notes. One of the drawbacks with tab is that it cannot accurately indicate rhythm. In order to play the right rhythms, you will probably need to listen to the song or review standard notation.

Individual numbers, which appear in a row on the staff, indicate single notes. Conversely, numbers stacked on top of each other indicate a chord or double stop (two notes played simultaneously). Sometimes the spacing may correlate to the actual rhythm but only crudely. Again, exact rhythmic specifications are beyond the scope of this type of notation. Tab is designed to show the positioning aspects of playing a melodic line or chord rather than the rhythmical aspects of that line. **FIGURE 3–4** shows some basic single-note tab patterns.

Tab is an evolving, creative, and dynamic tool. Increasingly, there are new ways to communicate complex and intricate performance techniques and articulations such as bends, slides, pull-offs, and so on. In the following chapters you will learn more about different techniques on the electric bass and how tab is used to notate them.

FIGURE 3–4.
Basic tab examples

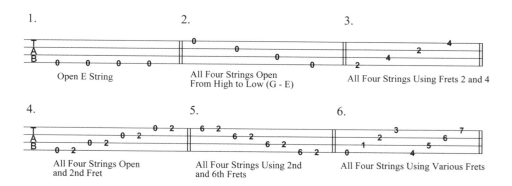

Understanding Rhythms in Standard Notation

All instrumentalists should understand rhythm since it is one of the basic elements of music. In standard notation, a note is made up of a note head and a note stem. A note head is seen either as an empty circle (whole or half notes) or as a colored-in dot (all other notes). A note stem is a vertical line that is attached to the note head. Sometimes notes are connected or barred together by a single horizontal line. This is used to indicate eighth notes. Sometimes you will see a double horizontal line. This is used to indicate sixteenth notes. Some single notes have a wavy line that curves down the stem. This is called a flag. A single flag is used to signify single eighth notes. A double flag is used to signify single sixteenth notes. All of these note types are shown in **FIGURE 3–5**.

FIGURE 3–5.

Types of notes

Whole   Half   Quarter   Eighth   Two Eighths   Sixteenth   Two Sixteenths

Notice that individual eighth notes look exactly the same as quarter notes but with a flag attached to it. The individual sixteenth note also looks like the quarter note but with two flags attached to it.

Table of Notes

Standard notation is based on mathematics, and it follows the same rules as fractions. **FIGURE 3–6** shows you the division of notes.

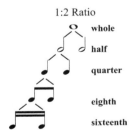

FIGURE 3–6.

The divisional relationship between notes moving from a whole note to a sixteenth note

As you can see, notes divide into two equal parts. A whole note divides into two half notes, a half note divides into two quarter notes, a quarter note divides into two eighth notes, and an eighth note divides into two sixteenth notes. When making these divisions, a 1:2 ratio occurs between the whole and half note, the half and quarter note, the quarter and eighth note, and the eighth and sixteenth note.

ALERT!

In the United Kingdom notes have different names. A whole note is called a *semibreve*, a half note a *minim*, a quarter note a *crochet*, an eighth note a *quaver*, and a sixteenth note a *semiquaver*. Don't be confused by this, and unless you live in England, don't use these terms.

the UK

The pie charts in **FIGURES 3–7** through **3–10** show the divisional relationship of notes.

You can see that two half notes equals the whole pie, four quarter notes equals the whole pie, eight eighth notes equals the whole pie, and sixteen sixteenth notes equals the whole pie. This is the mathematical backbone of notation.

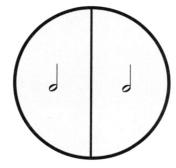

FIGURE 3–7.
Divisional foundation of notes—half notes

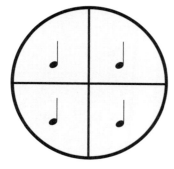

FIGURE 3–8.
Divisional foundation of notes—quarter notes

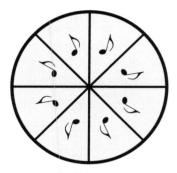

FIGURE 3–9.
Divisional foundation of notes—eighth notes

FIGURE 3–10.
Divisional foundation of notes—sixteenth notes

Rests

Rests function exactly the same way as notes but with one key difference. While a note signifies sound, a rest means silence. A rest does not mean to pause. The music continues whether you're resting or not (or whether there is sound or not). Think of a rest as a silent note.

When resting, always follow the music the same as if you were playing. Every note has a corresponding rest, and rests have the same relationship to one another as notes do. **FIGURE 3–11** shows each type of rest as it is divided from whole to sixteenth.

FIGURE 3–11.
Table of rests

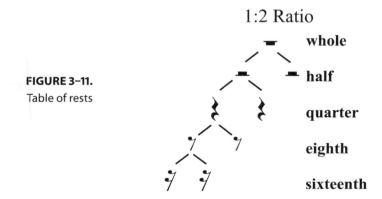

1:2 Ratio

whole

half

quarter

eighth

sixteenth

Time Signatures

Now that you have been exposed to notes and rests, you must piece them together to make rhythmical sentences. But in order to accomplish this, you must first learn about time signatures. There are many time signatures used in music; however, most of this book will focus on 4/4.

FACT

Another name for 4/4 is *common time*. If you turn the radio on and flip through the stations, you will hear 4/4 used on most songs. No other time signature is used so much in music. Part of the reason for this is the symmetrical nature of 4/4: 2+2 is easy to dance or groove to.

Understanding 4/4 Time

All time signatures contain a top number and a bottom number. These numbers tell the musician two important things:

- Number of beats in a measure (the top number)
- What note value equals one beat (the bottom number)

You're probably asking yourself, "What's a beat and what's a measure?" Most music is played in time; it has a pulse that, once started, continues until the tune reaches its end. This pulse is called the beat.

Notes and rests are segmented into smaller compartments of time. These boxes of time are called measures or bars. Notes and rests are contained within measures, and measure lines are used to mark each measure's borders. As **FIGURE 3–12** illustrates, measure lines—usually called bar lines—are simple vertical lines used to separate measures.

FIGURE 3–12.
Two measures
with bar line

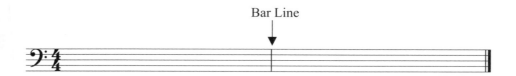

Bar Line

Think of 4/4 time as a fraction even though technically it is not. You will notice in standard notation that there is no line dividing the two number fours; the fours merely sit on top of one another. For educational purposes, temporarily accept 4/4 as a fraction.

All fractions have a top number called a numerator and a bottom number called a denominator. The numerator tells you how many beats you have in a measure. Since there is a four in the numerator, you can say that there are four beats in each measure.

The denominator tells you what note value equals one beat. In order to find this, temporarily replace the numerator with a one. Now, you have 1/4, or a quarter. This tells you that the quarter note equals the beat. So in 4/4, you have four beats in a measure, and the quarter note represents (or equals) each beat.

Quarter and Eighth Notes

Quarter notes function as the pulse or beat in most of the music you will play. Most of the music you will hear uses the quarter note as its heartbeat. When you place four quarter notes into a measure of 4/4, it is counted like **FIGURE 3–13**.

FIGURE 3–13.
Four quarter
notes

1   2   3   4

Each quarter note represents a downbeat. In 4/4, downbeats equal the numbers one, two, three, and four. If we divide quarter notes into eighth notes, we will have eight of them per measure. **FIGURE 3–14** shows one measure of eighth notes.

In **FIGURE 3–14** the beat was divided into two parts. It should be counted "one and, two and, three and, four and." The "ands" are called upbeats. Upbeats represent the second half of a beat.

FIGURE 3–14.
One measure of
eighth notes

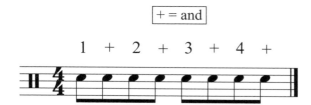

Keeping Time and Counting Out Loud

One of the most important facets of music is time keeping. Without a good internal clock, you will have limited ability to play with other musicians. Music exists in time and space. Time refers to the pulse of the music, while space refers to the rhythmical components (notes and rests) that exist within a time span.

All musicians should focus on time keeping, but this is especially true of bass players since you lay down the groove of the music. One of the best ways to improve your time and your overall sense for music is to count beats aloud. Professionals do not count out loud when they perform; however, counting is crucial in the practice room, especially for beginners. Counting will help you to make sense of the rhythms you are reading.

As previously stated, when you see four quarter notes you should count the downbeats one, two, three, four. Counting divisions and subdivisions are also helpful. For instance, you know that eighth notes are counted one and, two and, three and, four and. Sixteenth notes are counted using the syllables one-ee-and-ah, two-ee-and-ah, three-ee-and-ah, four-ee-and-ah. See **FIGURE 3–15**.

FIGURE 3–15.
Counting
sixteenth notes

No matter what, you must always count off before you begin playing. This applies to all styles of music. A tempo must be established before you begin playing a tune. Counting off solidifies the speed and helps to avoid unwanted tempo shifts as you play.

Chapter 4

Keys, Scales, and Technique Building

It's now time to really start playing the bass! First, get your bass up and running and your rig set up and ready to use. Next, make sure you tune your bass and get it in a proper, comfortable playing position. Once you do this, you are ready to familiarize yourself with some important notes on the bass. In this chapter you will learn basic patterns on each string. Additionally, you will be introduced to key signatures and major and minor scales.

4

Technique Builders: Part 1

The lowest pitched and thickest string is an E. It is sometimes referred to as the fourth string. Your first task is to play that string open. This means that you will play the string without depressing it on the fretboard with the left hand. When doing so, remember to use good technique when plucking or picking the string. Also, when plucking, always draw and release the string as described in Chapter 2.

It's important to strive for a good sound and tone when playing any instrument. When playing notes on a bass, try to make them sound round, full, and pleasant. By following good technical advice and listening critically to the sounds you are making, you can make subtle adjustments and gradually improve your tone until you sound like a pro.

After you've familiarized yourself with the open E string, you are now ready to play the first fret, which is F. F is found on fret one; it is the fret nearest the nut on the neck of the E string. Place the index finger of the left hand over and slightly behind the first fret and press the string down using your fingertip. Make sure to keep your fingers and hand in a rounded position with your left-hand thumb making a rounded clamp on the back of the neck. Next, pluck the note with your right hand. After this, try playing G on the third fret of the E string. To depress the string, use finger three—the ring finger—of your left hand.

The notes E, F, and G are found on the staff in **FIGURE 4–1**. They are played as whole notes.

Make sure to hold each note for four counts. At this stage, speed is not important. What is important is making sure the correct note is played and held for four, nearly clock-steady, counts. Timing is everything in music. So play steady and even, not necessarily fast.

Next, try playing quarter notes on the E string (**SEE FIGURE 4–2**). You may let the last note ring, hence the use of a whole note at the end of the phrase.

Quarter notes get only one count. Because quarter notes inherently move more quickly, make sure to choose a comfortable tempo (probably fairly slow) to play the exercise. Once you've mastered **FIGURE 4–2**, try an

FIGURE 4–1. E, F, and G notes on the E string

TRACK 1

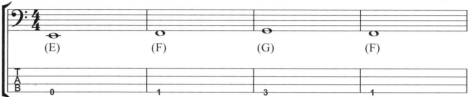

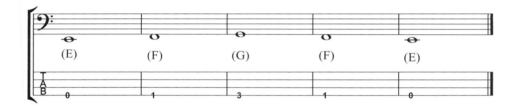

FIGURE 4–2. Quarter notes on the E string

TRACK 2

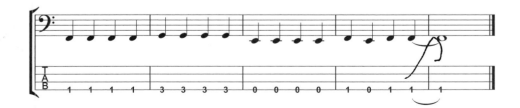

exercise that uses mixed note values. This means that the number of counts each note gets becomes mixed up. This is shown in **FIGURE 4–3**. Here you will use quarter and half notes until the end where two whole notes tell you to let the final note ring out.

FIGURE 4–3. Mixed note values

TRACK 3

Music educators can't emphasize enough the importance of making sure that each note is getting the precise amount of steady counts—no more or less than is indicated. At this stage, playing the right notes in the right time, with decent tone, is a grade A no matter how slow your tempo.

In the next section, **FIGURES 4–4** through **4–12** follow the same approach you used on the E string so that you can learn about the white notes (not sharped or flatted) on the instrument. However, this time you will be working off of the A, D, and G strings.

Additionally, **FIGURES 4–4** through **4–12** will help you build your knowledge of the fretboard, the bass clef, and rhythms. Further, they will help build some technique. In these figures and for the rest of the chapter, always use fingers one, two, and three on frets one, two, and three respectively. The only exception to this is when you play the G string.

If you don't press the string down hard enough in the left hand you will hear a buzzing sound when you play. The buzz can be avoided by pressing down on the fret with a little more force. With a little trial and error you will discover how much pressure you should apply in order to get a clean, buzz-free sound.

Playing on the A, D, and G Strings

As just mentioned, **FIGURES 4–4** through **4–12** give you a chance to practice playing on the A, D, and G strings. When plucking the strings, alternate as much as possible between your index and middle fingers. Some players even use their ring finger. When using a pick, make sure to use a downward (down pick) as well as upward (up pick) motion. This is accomplished by driving the pick through the string in an up or down alternating fashion.

FIGURES 4–4 through **4–9** concentrate on the A string:

FIGURE 4–4.
A, B, and C notes
on the A string

FIGURE 4-5.
Quarter notes on
the A string

FIGURE 4-6.
Mixed rhythms
on the A string

A dotted half note 𝅗𝅥. is worth three beats!

The following figures concentrate on the D string:

FIGURE 4–7.
D, E, and F notes on the D string

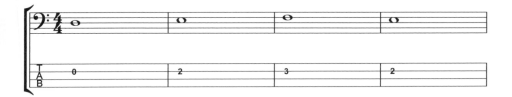

FIGURE 4–8.
Quarter notes on the D string

FIGURE 4–9.
Mixed rhythms
on the D string

In **FIGURES 4–10** through **4–12**, you will need to modify your left-hand fingering on the G string. Here you'll use finger one on fret two (A), finger three on fret four (B), and finger four, the pinky finger, on fret five (C). Fingering is always subject to revision, personal comfort, and musical necessity, and it can actually be a creative endeavor. For example, some bassists prefer to use the fourth finger in place of the third finger for most passages (like upright bassists often do).

FIGURE 4–10.
G, A, B, and
C notes on the
G string

FIGURE 4–11.
Quarter notes
on the
G string

FIGURE 4–12.
Mixed
rhythms on
the G string

Sharps and Flats

In the last section you learned the so-called *white notes* of the electric bass. They are called white notes because they correspond with the white keys on a piano. By now you should know where to find any white note in the musical alphabet, A through G, on the bass. You even know two options on each note found in differing octaves, with the exception of D. However, the musical alphabet is regularly modified by the use of halfway points (also known as half steps) between the alphabetical notes. These halfway points are better known as sharps or flats, depending on usage and musical context.

With the exception of B, C, E, and F, all the notes in the musical alphabet contain a sharp or a flat in between them. This sharp or flat represents a halfway point in pitch between each alphabetical pair of notes. On the bass guitar, this corresponds to the frets that fall directly between the white notes (also called naturals) that you learned earlier in the chapter. These sharps or flats correspond to the black notes on a piano. When playing these notes on the bass guitar fretboard, simply use the fingers that are adjacent to the fingers used to play the white notes. In other words, if you want to play a low F-sharp instead of F natural on the E string, use finger two since F-sharp falls between F natural and G natural, which use fingers one and three respectively.

In general, there are two ways to encounter sharps or flats in musical notation. First, you may see the sharp or flat written right next to the note on the staff. This is called an *accidental*. It is called an accidental because, in a sense, it is an accident—an accident whereby a note normally consonant in a given key is altered by sharping or flatting it. When it is sharped or flatted, it is taken outside the realm of the normal key.

Key Signatures

The second manner in which you will find sharps or flats is in a key signature. Here, sharps or flats are indicated at the beginning of each line near the clef. A sharp means to raise a note one half step (again, equal to one fret). A flat means to lower it one half step (or one fret). If you see a key signature, be sure to obey what it says. Sharps or flats in the key signature tell you to sharp or flat specific notes. For instance, if you see three sharps in the key signature (F, C, and G), you must always play the sharp of those notes instead of F, C, and G naturals. What do sharps or flats in the key signature look like? The sharps or flats are placed on the lines or spaces of the staff to the right of the clef. (You will see them later in the chapter.)

The order of sharps and flats and the theory behind key signatures can be a rather technical subject. For now just try to memorize the order of the sharps or flats using the following mnemonics. For sharps use *Fat Cats Get Dizzy After Eating Barley*, representing the order F, C, G, D, A, E, and B. The order of flats is B, E, A, D, G, C, and F, which can be remembered as *BEAD Go Call Fred*.

Another neat aspect of key signatures is that they are, just like a person's signature, the unique mark of whatever the key happens to be. When you see a key signature at the beginning of a piece of music, it is indicative of the key itself. There are some neat tricks that musicians use to figure out what major key they are in. First, if you have no sharps or flats, then you are in the key of C major. If you are given sharps, start by reading the name of the last sharp (the one furthest away from the clef sign). Once you've found the last sharp, add one half step to that specific note so that you have a second note. That second note is the name of the actual major key. For example, say the last sharp is C-sharp. One half step higher than C-sharp is D; therefore, you are in the key of D.

For flat keys, the formula is even easier. You are in the key of whatever happens to be the second to last (left to right) flat of the key signature. So if your key signature is four flats (B, E, A, D) you are in the key of A-flat. If all this is still a bit confusing, don't worry! You will gain more understanding of this topic in following chapters as you delve more and more into music theory.

Before you begin playing sharps or flats, take a moment to review all the notes you've learned so far. The next two figures will help you do just that. So far you've been playing in what is commonly known as first position. Soon you'll play further up the neck. For now, try what bassists commonly call the natural scale in first position. This scale has no sharps or flats (that is, it has only naturals.) See **FIGURE 4–13** for the natural scale and **FIGURE 4–14** for a review of what you've learned so far.

FIGURE 4–13.
The natural scale, first position

FIGURE 4–14. Review: Look at what you know!

TRACK 4

It's time to take a look at using some sharps or flats. The first sharp that you might encounter is F-sharp. F-sharp is commonly found in the key of G major (or its relative minor, E minor). You will find F-sharp on the second fret of the E string (use finger two) and the fourth fret of the D string (use finger three) as shown in **FIGURE 4–15**.

FIGURE 4–15.
Playing F-sharp

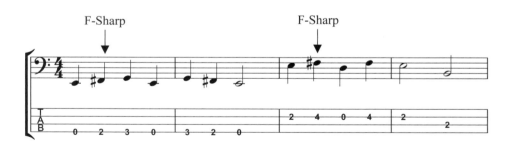

When using sharps or flats, you must remember the following rule: Once a sharp or flat is introduced in a measure, it holds for the *entirety* of that measure. For example, in **FIGURE 4–15**, beat three of measure seven is an F-sharp. Why? This is because an F-sharp was first introduced on beat two of the same measure.

Also, you may encounter B-flat. B-flat is commonly seen in the key of F major (or its relative minor, D minor). Play B-flat on the A string with finger one. Play B-flat on the G string with finger three. See **FIGURE 4–16**.

FIGURE 4–16.

Playing B-flat

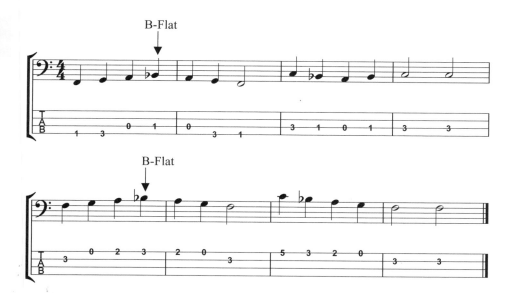

Major and Minor Scales

Getting comfortable with accidentals and key signatures, including knowing why and how to use each, is a complex matter. This is because the proper use of sharps and flats, and the basic concept of keys and key signatures, can really only be fleshed out by first understanding scales.

Scales tell you what it means to be *in* a given key. If you want to play in the key of E-flat major, the E-flat major scale is what makes the reality of that key explicit.

What is a *key*?

There are twelve musical notes in Western music. The term *key* means that one of those twelve notes becomes the tonal center in a piece of music. The key signature and the musical content and context indicate what note equals the key in a given piece of music.

In music, the name of the key's center and the first note of the scale are known as the *tonic*. Scales and keys are defined and named by tonic pitches. In fact, the tonic acts as the tonal center, or home base, for scales and keys. For example, if you are in the key of C, the note C will become the center of the musical universe. In this case, the other notes revolve around C and play a supporting role. You might think of C as the king in his castle and the rest of the notes as his subjects. But don't get confused. In the key of F, for instance, C becomes a subject and F becomes the king!

A scale is made up of seven different notes plus an eighth note that is a repetition of the tonic one octave higher. Usually performed in ascending and descending fashion, each note in a scale can be numbered indicating its position in the scale. These numbers are called scale degrees.

There is a relational aspect to all scales and keys that makes them essentially the same. All major and minor keys and scales are based on the same exact recipe, relatively speaking. That recipe is based on whole-step intervals (two frets apart) and half-step intervals (one fret apart). For major scales, the recipe is:

1. Play the tonic.
2. Go up one whole step (two frets) and play that note.
3. Go up another whole step (two frets) and play that note.
4. Go up a half step (one fret) and play that note.
5. Go up a whole step (two frets) and play that note.
6. Go up a whole step (two frets) and play that note.
7. Go up a whole step (two frets) and play that note.
8. Go up a half step (one fret) play that note.

Reverse to descend the scale. To summarize, the intervallic model for a major scale is whole, whole, half, whole, whole, whole, half. This is true in all keys.

Believe it or not, natural minor scales contain the same content as major scales. Only the intervallic order is changed. Consequently, every major scale has a relative minor. How do you find the tonic of a relative minor scale? All you need to do is find the sixth scale degree of its major scale partner. This is best learned through example.

In the key of C major, you would count up six steps to A. The steps are C, D, E, F, G, and A. A is the sixth scale degree; therefore, A minor becomes C major's relative minor key. Both scales, major and minor, share the exact same key signature. Only by listening or studying the content of the piece can you tell if it is in a major or minor key.

Technique Builders: Part 2

It's time to apply what you've learned so far in a more concrete way to playing the bass. In the following exercises, you will get a chance to hear, feel, and internalize the concepts just presented. These exercises will also advance your technique, your ear, and your overall musical vocabulary. **FIGURE 4–17** is a C-major scale notated for you. Notice how it conforms to the whole-whole-half-whole-whole-whole-half model described earlier.

FIGURE 4–17.

The C-major scale

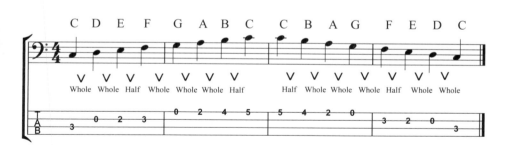

You should familiarize yourself with the sound of the major scale. Just like all natural colors are derived from the spectrum of visible light, melodies, bass lines, and harmonies are derived from the musical rainbow known as the major scale. Think of scales as musical number lines with each scale degree moving up a linear ladder of pitch. In music, the number line is turned into a loop where, at the octave, the end of the scale is fastened to the beginning again. In the scalar examples included here, you'll proceed up to this end and then reverse direction, descending back to the starting point.

FIGURE 4–18 shows how scales can translate into a melodic bass line. Notice that all of the notes used in this melody appear in the C-major scale.

FIGURE 4–18.
Melody in the
key of C major

Next is the relative minor of C major: A natural minor. This is shown in **FIGURE 4–19**. Notice that this scale uses the same alphabetical note content as the C-major scale. The only difference is that it's inverted so that it originates and terminates on A instead of C.

FIGURE 4–19.
The A-natural
minor scale

FIGURES 4–20 and **4–21** illustrate a G-major scale and E-natural minor scale. Again, the major scale uses the whole-half intervallic model described previously, and both scales use F-sharp in their key signatures. Notice that they have the same quality, soundwise, as the C-major and A-natural minor scales. Again, this is because they follow the exact same intervallic models. The only exception is the tonal center, or key. In other words, the anchor or home base is different. Remember: When playing these scales always use F-sharp, not F natural.

FIGURE 4–20.

The G-major scale

FIGURE 4–21.

The E-natural minor scale

Now try playing a scale that uses flats. **FIGURE 4–22** shows the F-major scale. Like all other major scales, it is based on the whole-whole-half-whole-whole-whole-half intervallic model.

FIGURE 4–22.

The F-major scale

Finally, try playing some etudes (study pieces) that utilize the G-major scale and A-natural minor scale respectively. The difficulty level is further augmented by the use of eighth notes and dotted quarter notes. Dotted quarter notes are worth one and a half beats. This is illustrated in **FIGURES 4–23** and **4–24**.

FIGURE 4–23. Etude in G major

TRACK 5

Dotted quarter notes ♩. are worth one beat *plus* another half beat!

+ = and

FIGURE 4–24. Etude in A natural minor

TRACK 6

Chapter 5

Harmony and Chord Progressions

In this chapter you will learn about the harmonic underpinning of music. Even though the electric bass is primarily a melodic (single notes) instrument, you will need to understand harmony in order to properly structure bass lines. *Harmony* is the simultaneous sounding of two notes. Harmony helps to propel the emotional component in music. It also works in tandem with the melodic content of a piece.

Intervals and Chord Basics

The most basic unit of harmony is an interval. An interval is the measured distance between any two notes. If two notes of the interval are played simultaneously, they form a harmonic interval. If they are played consecutively, they form what is known as a melodic interval. Melodic intervals can sometimes imply harmony, even though they are not officially harmonic. For example, if you break up a "chord" (another name for a distinct harmony) by playing each note separately but consecutively, you are playing what's known as an arpeggio or broken chord. Arpeggios have clear harmonic underpinnings.

Because of the specific acoustical relationships between particular notes, certain intervals create more consonant (pleasant) resonances than others. In general, the more consonant intervals form the basis of complex harmonies known as chords. The primary expression of harmony is generally regarded as the triad. Triads are three-note chords (or arpeggios) utilizing the consonant intervals of thirds and fifths. The alphabetical name and origin of a triad is known as its *root* and serves a similar function as the tonic of a scale or key except that the root grounds each chord regardless of the overall key. Half-step alterations to specific notes in the triad, excluding the root, result in variant chord types. In other words, through varying the intervals, you can take any set of three notes and make them major, minor, augmented, or diminished.

QUESTION?

What is a major or minor chord?
Major and minor triads are probably the most well-known chords. A major triad is composed of a root, a major third, and a perfect fifth. The major third gets its name because it is a major third interval above the root (or four half steps). The perfect fifth is a perfect fifth interval above the root (or seven half steps). To make the triad minor, simply drop the third interval by one half step. For example, C to E is a major third. To find the minor third, lower the E to an E-flat.

Major and minor chords are an important part of most music. They often evoke general emotions such as sadness, happiness, fear, or contentment. A major triad can often encourage positive emotions while minor triads are known to spark more negative connotations. As you more consciously recognize and compare the sounds of major and minor triads in use, you'll get a better sense of these possibilities. Try playing the triads in **FIGURE 5–1** to get a sense of what these chords sound like on the bass and how they can be played.

FIGURE 5–1.
Major and minor triads in G

Diatonic Chords

Another way to look at chords is to see them related to scales and keys. A given major scale or key represents a musical universe founded upon a chosen key center or tonic pitch. The tonic is the first note of a scale. It's also the name of the scale and its corresponding key signature. Once you choose your tonic pitch and key, it's then time to investigate what chords inhabit that musical realm.

Remember, each note in the scale can be numbered one through seven. This can often help you analyze, and even memorize, a certain succession of notes (melody) through the use of these scale degrees and intervals. Bringing a more harmonic emphasis into the picture, you can now build triads—or later, larger chords—on these same numbered scale degrees. Each note in the scale can have a chord that emanates from it. By choosing the notes for those chords only from the constituent members of the scale or key, you maintain the integrity of the key. When you create harmony out of the scale itself, you're employing what's called diatonic harmonization. Before you embark on this odyssey of harmony, it would be helpful if you'd review some major scale patterns on the electric bass. You should also learn the remaining notes on the neck.

You know that each open string on the bass (E, A, D, G) increases by one half step as you move fret by fret up the neck. For example, the E string proceeds as follows: open E, F, F-sharp/G-flat, G, G-sharp/A-flat, A, A-sharp/B-flat, B, C, C-sharp/D-flat, D, D-sharp/E-flat, E. Above the twelfth fret on each string, the notes simply repeat. All the strings proceed in a similar fashion.

When acquainting yourself with pitches on the neck, first identify where each white or natural note is on each string. Then, gradually fill in the sharps and flats. With the exception of E–F and B–C, the sharps and flats are always found in between the naturals on the neck.

When you have learned these important notes, you are now free to explore optional positioning of scales, exercises, and any other musical passage. Before you get too creative, first play a major scale that starts on a low G (third fret, E string) and moves all the way up the E string (see **FIGURE 5–2**). This gives you a chance to use the whole-whole-half-whole-whole-whole-half formula mentioned in Chapter 4. Since this is a G-major scale, there is one sharp found in the key signature (F-sharp). This means that you will always play F-sharps in this key unless otherwise notated.

Next, look at the tab for a major triad and minor triad on one string. Notice that the G-major triad and the A-minor triad use every other note found in the G-major scale, starting on the notes G and A respectively. This is illustrated in **FIGURE 5–3**.

FIGURE 5–2.
G-major scale on one string

Be mindful of the key signature!

FIGURE 5–3.
G-major triad and
A-minor triad on
one string

This should start to give you the idea of what diatonic triads are doing. Again, you take the major scale and build triads starting on each of its notes. Those triads further exploit the major scale by utilizing every other note within the scale as the basis for those triads. This also makes visible the form of the triad that employs the root-third-fifth formula.

Finally, take a look at a new position for the major scale. In **FIGURE 5–4**, you will use a closed position, meaning that no open strings are used to play this scale.

FIGURE 5–4.
G-major scale in
closed position 1

Be mindful of the key signature!

Next, diatonic triads can be attached to each note or scale degree using the new closed position major scale. As an additional challenge, try reading this exercise using standard notation instead of tab. Tab is provided in case you need help. Also, since the bass is such a symmetrical instrument, tuned in perfect fourths, you should notice that the upper G (the highest note in **FIGURE 5–4**) can also serve as a brand new starting point for extending the G-major scale beyond one octave to the next highest D. As stated earlier, chords played as single notes are called arpeggios or broken chords. This is shown in **FIGURE 5–5**.

FIGURE 5-5. G-major diatonic triads in closed position 1

TRACK 7

Be mindful of the key signature!

Functions, Roman Numerals, and Progressions

Diatonic triads that ascend the scale degrees in a given key are also called chord *functions*. Furthermore, these numbers, when applied to chords (instead of single notes of a scale) are written in Roman numerals. This numbering of chords within a key helps to provide a type of musical shorthand for musicians who are interested in studying the underlying harmonic content and movement of a piece of music. This movement is typically referred to as a chord progression.

Notice that the diatonic triads in **FIGURE 5–5** proceed as follows: G major, A minor, B minor, C major, D major, E minor, and F-sharp diminished. This pattern, which is the natural outcome of deriving chords from the G scale itself, is one that will be generated in any key. All major scale diatonic triads will progress as follows: major (I), minor (ii), minor (iii), major (IV), major (V), minor (vi), and diminished (vii).

Chord progressions can be rather simple or complex. Different kinds and eras of music hold to different standards of complexity. For instance, blues and early rock music often use merely three chords. Alternatively, modern jazz and most forms of classical music employ complex chord progressions. These chords may even extend beyond the given key and imply several keys all at the same time.

One advantage of using Roman numerals instead of alphabetical chord symbols is the fact that Roman numerals communicate relationships as opposed to absolute values. This means that they instantly communicate the underlying structure of the chord progression rather than seemingly arbitrary succession of chords. On the other hand, chord symbols are a more clear-cut, objective form of musical communication, and they are best employed when trying to actually play music (as opposed to analyzing it). You will learn more about standard chord symbols at the end of this chapter.

ALERT!

When writing major chords, always capitalize the Roman numerals, for example, IV or V. When writing minor chords, the Roman numeral is written in lowercase: iii or vi.

To get a taste of what it is like to think in Roman numerals look at **FIGURE 5–6**. Here, you will play broken triads using the Roman numerals I through vi. Included are the roman-numeral chord function symbols and the written notes. You can choose how to play these notes, but it is probably wise to use closed position 1 or some adaptation of it.

FIGURE 5–6.

Reading Roman numerals I, ii, iii, IV, V, and vi in G major

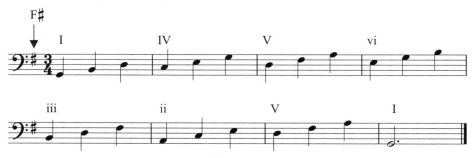

Uppercase Roman numerals indicate *major*. Lowercase Roman numerals indicate *minor*.

Recommended: Use the same closed position found in Figure 5-5.

The Role of Chords Within Keys

Each chord or chord function in a key is not created equal. You may have noticed that the I chord in **FIGURE 5–6** feels like home when you end on it at the end of the exercise. In a very real sense it is home! All the musical elements have conspired, in total, to psychologically construct that ending G to feel like home and to give a sense of emotional closure. Again, the basic element that manipulates your emotions comes from the fact that all the chord functions use the notes of this particular major scale (G major). Thus, the G chord is preeminent, and all the other chords play a more or less subordinate role. The I chord in any key will create the same emotional sense of closure as long as the key center is revealed through a series of chords that are related to the I chord's major scale. **FIGURE 5–7** illustrates this idea in the key of A major. When playing in this key, be sure to play F-sharps, C-sharps, and G-sharps.

The I chord is not the only chord to play a specific role in a progression. Sometimes the roles of the other chords are pronounced; sometimes they are concealed. In highly predictable pop music, or even classical, the other chord functions can behave in a stereotypical role, much the same way actors might in a drama. Because the vi chord is derived from the sixth scale degree and is the tonic of the relative minor (see Chapter 4), it can sometimes sound like the I chord's evil twin. This is especially true when it serves as the beginning of a new musical section. The IV chord can serve as a complement to the I chord, or a home away from home in many

FIGURE 5–7.
Reading
Roman
numerals I, ii,
iii, IV, V, and vi
in A major

This key signature (A Major) uses three sharps: F-sharp, C-sharp, and G-sharp.

circumstances. Other times, chord functions can have a push or pull effect to other chord functions. For example, the ii chord often likes to progress to the V chord, while the iii chord is often drawn to the vi or IV chords. These tendencies have at their core real theoretical underpinnings that will be discussed later on.

There are different conceptual frameworks that can serve both to analyze and inspire different kinds of chord progressions. Random chord progressions (I–iii–V–ii–vi–IV) seem to follow no discernable framework at all, although often, through closer inspection, fragments of some organization can be drawn out. *Linear* chord progressions tend to move up or down the musical alphabet's line, flowing in patterns that are segments or parts of a scale. A progression that goes upward (I–ii–iii–IV–V) is a good example. Anywhere there are two numbers that are neighbors, as in iii–ii or vi–V, you have a linear progression. Finally, there are progressions that move in intervals of fourths. Fourth progressions are probably the most common progression in all of music. A fourth interval up from any chord is also the same as going a fifth down from that same chord. Fourth progressions hop from one chord to the next according to the interval of a perfect fourth. For example, if you start on the iii chord, then you next go to the vi chord. Then you might go to the ii, then the V chord, and then finally the I chord.

FIGURE 5–8 uses three kinds of chord progressions. It also employs arpeggios or broken chords. Measures one through four employ linear progression concepts. Measures five through eight employ fourths progression concepts. Measures nine through sixteen employ a mixture of any or all of these as well as random chord progressions. Notice that you are still employing these in a manner consistent with the overall diatonic triad scheme presented earlier in this chapter.

FIGURE 5–8. Etude in F major—three kinds of chord progressions

TRACK 8

This key (F Major) uses one flat - B♭.

ALERT!

Remember, the musical alphabet is only seven letters long. If you number them one through seven, or I through vii for chords, and cycle through them, you will get a musical number line as follows: I, ii, iii, IV, V, vi, vii, I, ii, iii, IV, V, vi, vii, and so on. So the progression (iii–vi–ii–V–I) simply moves through a cyclical musical number line *inclusively* by fours.

The Dominant Chord

In the previous section you learned about chord progressions in fourths. What makes these progressions so compelling (and ubiquitous) is that they exploit the concept of dominance. *Dominant* chords are those chords that lie a fifth interval away from a given chord. As mentioned previously, the intervals of fourths and fifths are the same except that they are inverted. That is, a fourth interval up from any chord is also the same as going a fifth down from that same chord, and a fifth interval up from any chord is the same as going down a fourth from that same chord.

Dominant chords are something of musical magic. Like the two opposite poles on a magnet, the pull between two ends of a perfect fifth interval is one of the greatest forces in Western music. The interval of a fifth is actually a stable force when played as a harmonic interval, but it is a propulsive force when played in melodic succession from V to I. When diatonic triads or more complex chords are played in likewise succession, you can hear the same force that propelled classical composers like Haydn and Beethoven to obsess on this progression at the end of almost every piece composed in the classical and early Romantic eras.

FIGURE 5–9 illustrates the pull toward the tonic that the V–I chord progression exhibits. Here, this exercise is referencing both the pull of the fifth within each chord to its tonic and the pull of the V chord itself to the I chord.

The strength of the relationship between the tonic and fifth, and the I chord and V chord, is particularly important for budding musicians to understand. In general, remember that everything in music is relative and connected in some way. For example, the V chord has its own V chord (called a V of V), and the two can be paired up for additional harmonic color.

FIGURE 5–9.

Hearing and feeling fifths

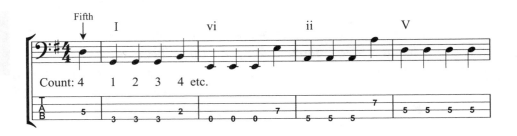

Notice that beat four in every bar contains the fifth of the following note.

Reading Basic Chord Symbols

When playing certain musical styles, it may be necessary to read chord charts. It is also a very handy method for learning the building blocks of a song. Chord symbols can be confusing at first, but with a little practice you'll be reading them in no time. Following are the elements:

- The alphabetical name of the chord (for example, C, G, or B-flat)
- The chord quality (for now only major or minor will be used)
- Chordal extensions (such as minor seventh, major seventh, major ninth, and so on; you will learn about these in Chapter 7)

In order to make sense of chord symbols, you should practice arpeggiating chords. **FIGURE 5–10** diagrams diatonic intervals as seen on the neck of the bass.

Notice that there are several ways to find major and minor thirds. This is shown in **FIGURE 5–11**.

Play the chords in **FIGURE 5–11** using the root or name of the chord on beat one of the measure. Use major or minor thirds on beat two; assume the third is major unless you see a "min" for minor. On beat three you will play a

FIGURE 5–10.
Reviewing
intervals

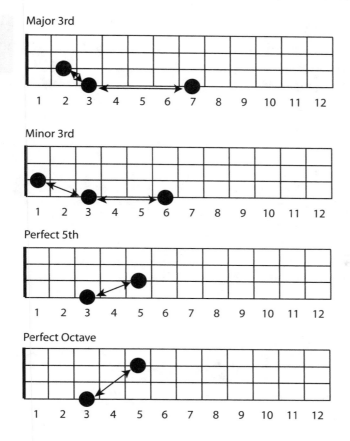

Major 3rd

Minor 3rd

Perfect 5th

Perfect Octave

FIGURE 5–11.
Playing thirds
in different
positions
within a triad

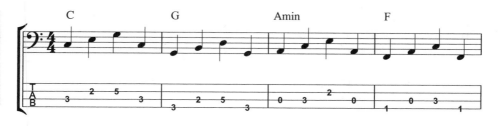

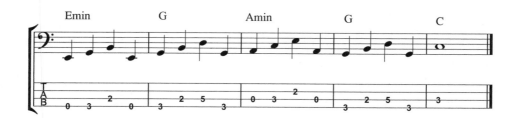

fifth, and on beat four you will play another root. Again, you play a root on beat one, a third on beat two (major or minor), a fifth on beat three, and a root on beat four.

Lastly, in **FIGURE 5–12** switch the fifth to beat two and the third to beat three. Try playing these notes in different positions and octaves.

FIGURE 5–12. Practice makes perfect

TRACK 9

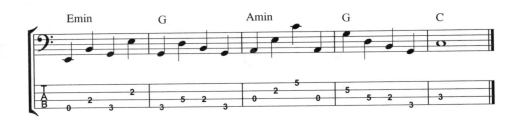

Chapter 6

The Role of the Bass

In this chapter you will learn about the role of bass in the rhythm section. More specifically, you will learn how to work with other musicians, sensitize yourself to a variety of grooves and musical environments, and develop an approach to playing, which will help you sound like a pro. So much of music making comes down to how you conceive of music— it's not just the notes you play.

The Rhythm Section

The bass is a member of the rhythm section. This term comes from an earlier period in popular music when swing orchestras dominated the scene and dance bands consisted of a rhythm section, a brass section, and a woodwind section. These days, most pop groups consist only of a rhythm section plus a singer(s). Nonetheless, the term *rhythm section* is still in use.

A rhythm section is composed of bass, drums, piano, and guitar. You do not need all four instruments to create a rhythm section. In other words, some rhythm sections consist only of a bass and a piano or a bass and a drum set. Whatever the combination, the rhythm section is responsible for the rhythmical and the harmonic underpinning of the music. In short, the rhythm section backs up or accompanies singers and soloists. The role of the bass in the rhythm section is twofold:

- To define and maintain the pulse and groove of the music
- To highlight the root of each chord

As you learned in Chapter 5, a root is the letter name of each chord. For example, the root of a C-major triad is a C. A good bass player knows how important it is to create bass lines that stress the roots even when playing intricate lines. Do you have to play every root? No. There is some wiggle room. However, you must be judicious and frugal when sidestepping the root. You should avoid roots only when a bass line or lick is compelling enough to temporarily sway the ear in another direction. Also, bass players sometimes experiment with alternate roots, adding extra harmonic sparkle to the chord changes.

For all intents and purposes, piano and guitar share the same responsibility in the rhythm section. They are the chordal instruments. When they play with a bass player, these instruments don't always plays roots, so, again, it's important for the bassist to play roots. If the bass doesn't, the music will lose its anchor and drift into a state of ambiguity, even confusion.

The drummer is the timekeeper. Together with the bass, the drums hold down the fort. The bass and drums work together to ensure steadiness and forward momentum in the music. In rock and pop, the bass and the bass drum (sometimes called kick drum) even play in tandem most of the time. Bass players and drummers share a special symbiotic relationship.

What Is a Bass Line?

Now that you understand the roles of each instrument in the rhythm section, it's time to bring the focus back to knowing more precisely what you will be doing. You have to play your part, but what is it?

If you are covering a song, you simply have to learn the part on the record or read some sort of provided notation. However, if you are in a more creative ensemble, where original compositions are being developed, you might have to create your own part.

FACT

Technically, a *bass line* is any part that a bassist plays, but often it consists of a repeated melodic pattern, or several of them, each representing the different sections that a piece of music might have. As a way to develop your ear, try picking out the different bass lines that comprise each section in one of your favorite songs.

If you will be simply performing a bass line that has already been recorded or composed, there are certain standards that you should consider. Do you want to play the bass part note for note as written, or do you want to take some liberties and add some improvisation? This decision is almost always dictated by the genre of music you will be performing.

If you are playing jazz or blues, you are usually expected to take chord changes or partially written notes and turn them into a more compelling part based on improvisation. Conversely, if you find yourself playing music that is more akin to classical music, you may need to stick more closely to the written score. Rock and its subgenres often have a broader range of performance expectations depending on which subgenre you are playing. For example, if you are playing Rush cover tunes, you probably will be expected to play the bass lines exactly as written. However, if you're in a jam band, you're obviously supposed to jam, meaning to improvise prodigiously.

There are often greater musical challenges if you are lucky enough to play in an original band. If you are allowed to create your own bass lines, it may be quite a challenge at first. So where do you begin?

You have to have the smarts to really understand just what kind of ensemble you are playing in and what kind of expectations the other musicians have. At the same time, you need to please yourself too. In general, bassists must play with empathy and generosity, and they have to enjoy backing up singers and soloists. Yes, bassists are featured on certain selections, and yes, select bassists consistently grab the spotlight. But usually the singer takes top billing in a rock or pop setting.

After you've thought about what it is you need to do stylistically, get some nuts and bolts information about the song. You'll need to determine what key or keys you'll be playing in, what the chords in the tune are, and what the rhythmic groove is. Subsequently, you'll fill the void with elements like root notes, other chord tones, scales, and arpeggios. As you work your way through this book, you will learn more and more about how to build appropriate bass lines.

Playing with a Drummer

Bass and drums are jointly responsible for the groove and feel of music. In rock and pop, the groove is usually defined by backbeats on beats two and four. In jazz, groove usually translates to mean swing. In Latin, the groove can take the form of a samba, a rumba, a soca, a merengue, or another rhythmical dance style. No matter what type of groove you're playing, the bass and the drums share the role as groove doctors.

Obviously, playing well with a drummer is essential. If you're not in sync with the drummer, the entire band will sound lackluster or even sloppy. In worst-case scenarios, the band will fall apart completely.

FIGURES 6–1 and **6–2** show a simple example of how the bass drum and bass guitar typically sync or lock up in a pop or rock milieu using a simple

FIGURE 6–1. Bass drum pattern

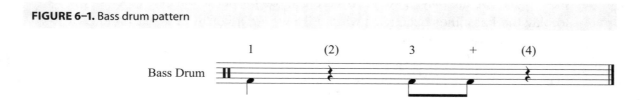

twelve-bar blues. The main rhythmical motif played by the bass drum is illustrated in **FIGURE 6–1**.

FIGURE 6–2.

Drum and bass etude

TRACK 10

In **FIGURE 6–2** you will see the bass drum and bass guitar playing in tandem on the main ostinato (see **FIGURE 6–1**) and also as the playing becomes more involved (measures nine through twelve). Be careful of the syncopated eighths used in bar ten. To help you out, the counting for this measure has been included.

QUESTION?

Does the bass guitar always have to sync up with the bass drum?
No. The two instruments simply have to be sensitive and aware of what the other is playing. In pop, and often in Latin music, the bass drum and bass guitar usually play ostinatos (repeated patterns) together. However, the bassist and drummer sometimes diverge rhythmically or play patterns that are similar and complementary but not exact. It all depends on the context and the songwriter's intentions.

Playing with Piano and Guitar

A good place to start getting your *chops*, or musical technique, together is in smaller ensembles. By playing with a fellow musician, even with a single guitarist or pianist, you can often find a level of intimacy and confidence that will help you make advancements. Besides that, it is often easier to coordinate schedules, which is a real concern in the music world. Nevertheless, one of the best aspects of performing in a small group setting is the lack of a dedicated timekeeper. Without a drummer, you are forced to confront the issue of time keeping in a more central way. In other words, you need to be more active in creating the groove and maintaining its tempo and feel.

As mentioned earlier, the first rule of bass playing in most genres of music is to establish the root of the chord. This is played on beat one of each measure or at the moment each new chord is struck. On the other beats, you generally fill in with complementary riffs (arpeggios, rhythmical patterns, and so on) or scalar passages. If you look back to Chapter 5, you'll see that the root note is always on beat one in each figure. It's singularly important to play these exercises (and the other exercises in this book) in time. This includes getting to the next measure in time.

Luckily, in most rock bands there is a guitarist. Having a guitarist in the band is great because you will, basically, speak the same musical language and you can help each other to stay in time. Your two instruments are not all that different. Because the tuning and layout of both instruments is similar, you can also show each other musical parts through visualization. In music, this type of communication is priceless.

FACT

The six-string guitar and the four-string bass are tuned similarly. In fact, the lowest four strings on the guitar are tuned to the same pitches as the bass. The only difference is that the strings on the guitar sound one octave higher. Also, the positioning and anatomy of the neck on the guitar parallels the bass.

The piano is often considered the most comprehensive instrument. This is because its pitch range is so vast and because polyphony (the ability to simultaneously play notes) is unlimited. The piano is a veritable symphony of sound. Also, the layout of the piano is like a visual map of the musical universe. By studying the piano, all musicians, including bassists, can get a better sense of the possibilities and implications of harmony, melody, and rhythm.

Similarly, playing with a good pianist can also be an education in itself. Pianists can often instruct you in the proper usage of chords, and they can easily supplement your bass part with chords and melody. There is not much a piano, in the right hands, can't do. This means that you can feel what it's like to play with a much larger ensemble even if it's just you and a pianist.

Playing Behind, in the Middle, and Ahead of the Beat

This book has already talked a lot about time. But what really is time? If you use a metronome (see Chapter 15) you will realize that time is a strict and rigid pulse. However, your playing should be fluid and graceful, not mechanical. So how do you play in time and yet avoid stiff playing? In order to do this, you need to create the illusion of playing loose all the while maintaining near-metronomic time. In order to do this, you will need to understand what it means to play behind, in the middle, and ahead of the beat. Moreover, you should learn how to play all three ways.

Some styles of music naturally sound like they have a lot of push or forward momentum; others naturally sound logy or relaxed. The first step in playing any style of music is to understand the nature of the music. Ballads or slow songs naturally want to sound relaxed and placid. In order to execute slower material, you should play slightly on top of the beat. If you don't, the music might start to drag or protract. There is nothing worse than a lazy tempo that runs out of steam altogether.

Up-tempo bluegrass tunes, bebop charts, or other fast pieces usually require you to play straight down the middle of the beat. If you play a little behind the beat, the music might start to drag. Conversely, if you play on top of the beat, the music might rush or speed up. If the song is already lightning fast, the last thing you'll want to do is to make it faster. This is because the faster you play the harder it is to maintain clean technique. If you rush on a fast tune, you will unwittingly sabotage your own playing.

Certain styles of rock music require you to play a little behind the beat. Select late-period Beatles tunes, funk and soul music, and nearly everything the Rolling Stones recorded uses a kind of behind-the-beat groove. Also, select blues shuffles and New Orleans swamp blues requires that you play on the back end of the beat. Playing behind the beat creates that phat, funky sound that makes these styles of music so infectious and popular. Other styles of music like punk and ska require you to play on top of the beat. When you play these styles, your playing should have an impatient, urgent feel to it. The excitement of these styles comes from the high-octane drive of the rhythm section.

How do you play behind, in the middle, or on top of the beat? Since this cannot be notated, the only way to learn how to do this is to listen to music with an ear toward feel, groove, and time extrapolation. As you listen, analyze how each style is interpreted and rendered by the bassist and drummer. Above all else, remember that playing behind or ahead of the beat doesn't mean overtly dragging or rushing. It simply means gently pushing or relaxing the time respectively.

Using Taste to Back Up Singers and Soloists

As previously mentioned, bassists are usually relied upon to play a supporting role. This is just the unvarnished truth. Although some electric bassists have developed their skills to such an advanced degree that they can transcend these limits (Jaco Pastorius and Victor Wooten are two examples), most bassists are relegated to an accompanying role. What often separates the best, in-demand bassist from the lesser player is one simple trait: taste.

Some players seem to always know what to do. Others seem to make their fellow musicians feel musically crowded. No musician wants to play with someone who doesn't have musical courtesy. This musical courtesy, or empathy, can take the form of keeping the volume of your amp at an appropriate setting or laying down a bass line that sends the right signals to a soloist. In general, some bassists intuitively know how to approach ensemble playing while others don't. Often young players have not developed all the musical character to know what to do. Musicians call these inexperienced players "green," just like rookies in sports. What can be done to make the less experienced player sound like the seasoned veteran? Here are some secrets:

- **Listen, listen, and listen.** You need to hear what everyone in the band is playing. If you can't hear the other musicians, you can't contribute in a meaningful way.
- **Turn down.** You should try to play as quietly as you can get away with.
- **Keep great time.** Everyone needs to stay in sync. If you play with great time, and your groove is solid and confident, you will be an asset to the group.
- **Know your parts.** Execute your bass lines with confidence and style.
- **Know when to let the other guy shine.** Don't fight for attention. You'll get your turn.
- **Know when it is your turn.** When it is your turn, don't solo endlessly. Improvise as elegantly and succinctly as you can, then happily resume your role as accompanist.
- **Have fun!** Remember the audience and your fellow musicians are feeding off of your vibe. Keep it positive!

A great way to learn the ropes is by performing with other seasoned musicians, especially great vocalists and hot soloists. Often these musicians understand that music is a mixture of art and commerce, and they excel at both. By feeding off of more experienced musicians you can learn how to captivate both the music aficionado and the average listener.

Chapter 7

Rock, Pop, and Country

In this chapter you will learn about the history of rock music, including its unique relationship to other styles such as R & B, blues, and country and western. You will also get introduced to rock's preeminent bassist, Paul McCartney. Additionally, you will learn practical bass lines that use roots, fifths, major and minor thirds, major and minor sevenths, and major sixths. The chapter ends with an introduction to alternate tunings, including how to play in drop D.

A Brief History of Rock

Shortly after World War II, the Jazz Age declined and a new form of music began to take shape. This new style culled from the race records of the rural South and the urban blues of Chicago. It also borrowed from country and western styles and later from politically charged folk music.

When rock-and-roll emerged in the early 1950s, it forever changed the face of popular music. Rock-and-roll gained in popularity due in large part to the development of the electric guitar, jukeboxes, television and the 45 rpm record. Key figures such as Alan Freed, Sam Phillips, Jerry Leiber, Mike Stoller, and others all took advantage of this technology by drawing white audiences and musicians alike to participate in the birth of a new era.

Music historians usually cite rhythm and blues (R & B) as rock's most important antecedent. Yet while R & B was predominantly black, rock's first superstar was Elvis Presley, a white kid from Tupelo, Mississippi. Presley blended gospel and country with a hefty dose of the blues and a spirited backbeat. The result was an infectious and energetic brand of rock-and-roll called rockabilly. Sam Phillips's record label, Sun Records, had a major impact on the rise of this style by signing Presley and assembling what would later be known as the Million Dollar Quartet, featuring Jerry Lee Lewis, Carl Perkins, Johnny Cash, and Presley.

Race had an enormous impact on the development of rock-and-roll and its stylistic forerunners. Jerry Wexler at Atlantic Records coined the term "rhythm and blues." His goal was to replace the label "race records," which was seen as an increasingly negative description of music made by black artists in the 1940s and 1950s.

Early rock-and-roll may have borrowed from many styles, but it was also inimitable in its own right. For instance, rock was attitude oriented, and it rebelled against the establishment. Further, rock used heavier backbeats, and it relied on amplification to get a larger-than-life sound. Rock's practitioners also often engaged in suggestive dancing on stage. Additionally, rock songs tended to be hook-laden, and they avoided the usual AABA song forms employed by composers of the Great American Songbook tradition.

Rock-and-roll made its crossover to white audiences when Elvis recorded "That's Alright Mama" in 1954, though he wouldn't earn a number one hit until 1956 with "Heartbreak Hotel." By the 1960s, rock would drop its "roll" and mature into a whole range of substyles due to the influence of such icons as Jimi Hendrix, the Who, the Rolling Stones, Bob Dylan, and, of course, the Beatles.

Paul McCartney is one of rock's great bassists. His band, the Beatles, is also one of the most influential rock/pop groups in history. In fact, they have become a musical institution. In his early period, McCartney's playing was more straightforward and simple. He used a lot of roots and fifths, like you'd find in country music. As the Beatles' music matured, McCartney's playing became more melodic and scalar.

In 1964, with the arrival of the Beatles on American shores, rock music firmly imbedded itself into the collective consciousness of society and has never left. Rock was dealt a harsh blow when rap and hip-hop topped it in CD sales in the 1990s, but it continues to thrive and have an enormous impact on popular culture. It is doubtful that rock will ever cease to be played.

Country and Western

Country and western helped to give birth to rock-and-roll. Country and western (C & W) is a pat term used to describe many different substyles of music. Most of these styles are regional. For example, Texas swing and Appalachian mountain music are two distinct genres found in the west and east respectively. However, despite regional distinctions, there is a lot of cross-pollination between such substyles as honky-tonk, Bakersfield sound, Nashville sound, outlaw country, and especially alternative country and country rock.

Country and western is one of America's truest art forms, though it has roots in European folk music, especially Anglo-Celtic fiddle music and ballad singing. Country is also influenced by blues and African American gospel music. (For more information on the blues see Chapter 8.)

Key innovators in country and western include cowboy crooners Roy Rogers and Gene Autry, bluegrass virtuosos Bill Monroe and Earl Scruggs, Texas troubadour Ernest Tubb, swing bandleader Bob Wills, guitar legend Chet Atkins, outlaw stylists Johnny Cash, Willie Nelson, and Waylon Jennings, and female vocalists Patsy Cline, Kitty Wells, Loretta Lynn, and Dolly Parton. However, the two biggest pioneers in country are Jimmie Rodgers, an early folk singer and yodeler, and Hank Williams, Sr., a legendary honky-tonk singer-songwriter.

Early country music used upright or acoustic bass. Today the electric bass is used in many styles of country. (The most notable exception is neo-traditional country spearheaded by Alison Krause, Ricky Scaggs, and others.) So much of country bass playing is founded on roots and fifths. Many of these types of bass lines are featured throughout this book. Sometimes the standard four-string bass is supplemented or replaced in recordings by a baritone guitar, also called a tic-tac bass. Modern electric country rock uses the same pop bass lines you will find in other Top 40 genres. Be sure to see Appendix A for information on essential country bassists.

Simple Patterns to Get You Rockin'

Rock can be the simplest form of music to play or it can be extremely complex. Even within one song, the difficulty level might shift dramatically. But when you are just starting out, it's best to keep it simple. Believe it or not, one of the most important grooves or bass lines in all of rock is the steady eighth note on the root of the chord. Also, steady quarter notes in a similar fashion are commonplace. In **FIGURE 7–1**, you'll be playing chord root notes in quarter notes and experimenting with octave shifts. Shifting the octave up or down is an easy way to give emotional lift or heft to something as simple as root notes. Among others, Paul McCartney was a genius at using this technique. Play the quarter notes from **FIGURE 7–1** in a pop style by making them short and snappy. This technique is known in music as *staccato* and marked with a dot below or above the note's head.

FIGURE 7–1. Pop quarter-note roots using octaves

TRACK 11

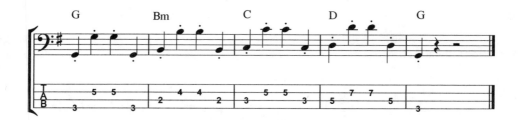

Here is that famous eighth-note groove mentioned earlier. **FIGURE 7–2** employs one of the easiest and most common rock bass lines. Play this groove with a driving feel and keep it steady and rocking. Hard rock and metal players often use this kind of bass line to propel their brand of rock.

FIGURE 7–2. Heavy metal eighth-note roots

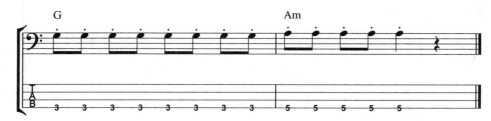

The dot over each note tells you to play short and staccato!

The next note to bring into the mix is the perfect fifth (see **FIGURE 7–3**). You've used this before so it should be familiar. However, expanding on the concept of octaves, you can use that same symmetry to locate a fifth below the root note as well as above it. Early rock and especially country music use a pattern where the root commences on beat one and the fifth hits on the third beat. Play **FIGURE 7–3** in a legato fashion, meaning to connect the notes by holding them out for their full beat value. Also, when playing legato it's important to make a smooth transition to the next note. In other words, there should not be any silence in between notes.

FIGURE 7–3. Using fifths and playing legato

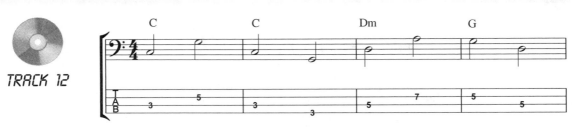

TRACK 12

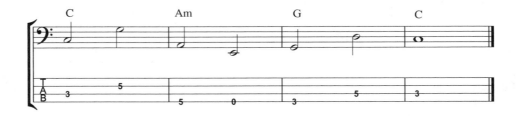

Staccato and legato are opposite kinds of musical articulations. Staccato means to play the note short and without sustain; legato means to make a seamless transition from one note to the next. Usually when playing legato you will also hold a note out for its full count; this is called tenuto. Staccato is marked with a small dot; legato is marked with a slur or arced line placed over or under a group of notes.

Notice that by varying the placement of the fifth it brings variety to the bass line even though the content is essentially the same. Just like with octaves, excitement can be generated by truly simple acts of variation. If you were given chord changes, you should now be able to construct a bass line similar to these exercises by using roots and fifths and staccato and legato techniques.

You just learned how to use octaves to move the fifth below the root of the chord. This can be done with any note in a chord. Wherever a note normally lies, remember to go up and higher two strings and frets or go down and lower two strings and frets. **FIGURE 7–4** shows you how to use other notes of the chord in a bass line. In this instance, you're working with roots and major and minor thirds. As you will see, some of the thirds are found in the octave below the root.

FIGURE 7–4.
Employing major
and minor thirds

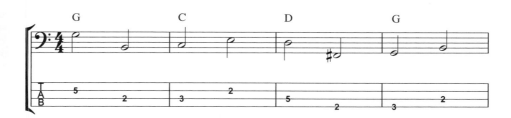

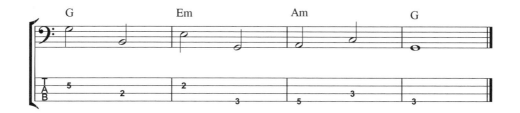

Adding Some Spice Through Chord Extensions

Your first introduction to playing chords dealt with learning triads. That was an important step. However, chords can become more complex and expressive than a mere three-note triad. In fact, part of the true beauty of music comes from the expression of harmonically rich chords that use extensions. The first note that crosses this threshold is the almighty seventh.

There are two types of seventh chords: the major seventh and the minor seventh. The minor seventh can also be called a dominant seventh. To avoid confusing the minor seventh and the minor triad, it is often best to use the name "dominant seventh" when describing the seventh scale degree as part of a dominant chord.

QUESTION?

How do I find the major seventh and minor (dominant) seventh?
The major seventh is ten half steps above the root of the chord. It is also found a half step below the root. The dominant seventh is nine half steps above the root of the chord or a whole step below it.

To learn seventh intervals on the bass, play the notes in **FIGURE 7–5**, which alternate between the root and the seventh. Here the seventh is used first as a major seventh (written as *maj. 7*) then as a dominant seventh (written as *7*). These are used a lot by more harmonically advanced rock bassists.

FIGURE 7–5.
Major and dominant sevenths

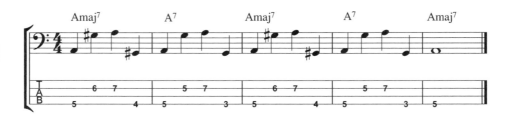

You need to incorporate this new chord extension back into the basic broken chord you learned earlier. In **FIGURE 7–6** you'll be using arpeggios to articulate four new varieties of seventh chords. As you will see, you can combine both major and minor triads with major and dominant sevenths.

You can see that both types of triads (major and minor) can contain two kinds of sevenths (major and dominant) attached to them. Be especially

FIGURE 7–6. Four types of seventh chords

careful when reading the chord symbols here. You'll want to study the symbols until you see how each chord is represented.

Another chord extension that becomes important, especially in the blues and in blues rock, is the major sixth. This extension is actually the same as an interval called a thirteenth. Depending on context and taste, you may see either name used. Again, to learn the intervallic placement of this note, it's best to look at it in rotation with the root. **FIGURE 7–7** does this both above and below the root by applying octaves.

ALERT!

It is crucial to understand that a "min" refers to the triad being minor while "maj" refers to the seventh being major. This is very confusing at first. If you temporarily use brackets, you will get a better picture of what is being modified: C (maj7) equals a C-major triad with a major seventh; C (7) equals a C-major triad with a dominant seventh, Cm (maj7) equals a C-minor triad with a major seventh, and Cm (7) equals a C-minor triad with a dominant seventh.

FIGURE 7–7.
Adding the sixth

F♯ is the sixth scale degree up from A!

FIGURE 7–8 is an arpeggio that uses the sixth, and it also sounds just like a familiar early rock-and-roll or R & B bass line. It's neat how something so emblematic of a certain style of music is based so directly on one single arpeggio (with variation).

FIGURE 7–8.
Arpeggiating
the sixth

Alternate Tunings

These days, modern rockers are experimenting with everything from crazy effect pedals to six-string bass guitars. A great way to expand your range on the instrument and to approximate five- or six-string basses is to experiment with alternate tunings.

A common tactic is to lower the E string by a whole step. This is a popular alternative tuning with some bassists who play hard rock or metal. By lowering the pitch of any guitar, it makes the tone sound deeper and heavier. Naturally, this is a good fit for heavy metal. If you want to try this, drop the E to a D and give **FIGURE 7–9** a try. In this figure, you'll play D, E-flat, F, and G on the open, first, third, and fifth frets respectively.

Some rock bands prefer to drop all the strings. For example, Van Halen likes to drop their guitars by one half step so that the tuning is E-flat, A-flat, D-flat, and G-flat. Objectively speaking, this is a detuning. But for all intents and purposes, they might as well consider themselves still in standard tuning since both the bass and guitar are equally detuned.

Through experimenting with alternate tunings, new creative and expressive possibilities may open up. The only thing that is recommended is that, for the most part, you stay conscious of the real note you are playing. You should also always know the interval name or that note's relationship to the chord you are on.

FIGURE 7–9.

Playing in drop D

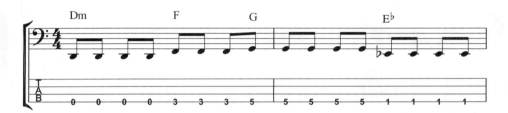

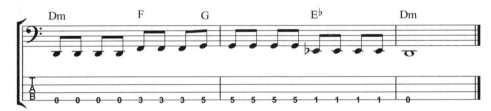

For this figure, don't forget to detune the E string to a D!

Chapter 8
Blues and Jazz

In this chapter you will learn about the history of blues and jazz as well as the basic elements of each style. As you will see, both styles are inextricably connected, and the bass guitar plays an important role in both genres. Additionally, you will get introduced to Jaco Pastorius, one of the most celebrated bassists of all time. Finally, you will begin constructing jazz and blues bass lines and learn about pedal tones, ostinatos, and harmonics.

A Brief History of the Blues

To understand the blues, you have to go back to slavery and the struggles of black Americans after the Civil War. In this climate, the blues was born. It comes from appalling work conditions on cotton and tobacco plantations and in the timber, turpentine, and levee camps of the Deep South. Ultimately, it is the story of oppression and unyielding racism.

Blues melodies, singing styles, structures, and rhythms can all be traced back to the tribal music of West Africa. Griot singing influenced the blues the most. Griot singers are storytellers. They typically do not perform in groups, only as soloists. They also accompany themselves on a stringed instrument not unlike the acoustic guitar.

The Mississippi Delta is considered the birthplace of the blues since it was here that the blues was first documented around 1900. Blues historians cite Charley Patton (1891–1934) as a key figure in the development of the blues. Some even call him the founding father. Clearly, Patton influenced blues legends such as Son House, Robert Johnson, Howlin' Wolf, John Lee Hooker, and a whole host of others.

Prior to W. C. Handy (1873–1958), the blues was played only in the American South. However, Handy transformed the blues from a backwoods style of music to a new form of entertainment that could be bought, sold, and mass marketed. By the 1920s, musicians of all races were performing and recording the blues. The blues could be heard on concert stages and on 78 rpm recordings distributed by record labels such as Victor, Okeh, the American Record Corporation, and Paramount.

After both world wars, black musicians from the Mississippi Delta moved to northern cities such as Detroit and Chicago. This was called the Great Migration. When Delta musicians arrived in Chicago they began using amplifiers, and soon the legendary Chicago style was born. The Chicago style of blues was a direct precursor to rock-and-roll. It was also one of the first genres to embrace the electric bass.

Today the electric bass is commonly used in blues-rock, a hybrid that is played throughout the nation. Blues-rock is a potpourri of styles, and it is an excellent vehicle for bassists who like to play shuffle rhythms, walking bass lines, and ostinatos. You will learn all about these terms later in the chapter.

A Brief History of Jazz

As early as 1895, jazz was emerging in New Orleans. Early jazz blended the syncopated rhythms of ragtime with the harmonic elements of the blues and the raw energy of New Orleans marching bands. The most salient feature of jazz was its use of improvisation. The spontaneity of this music and the colorful nature of many of its early practitioners made jazz captivating. Before long it was thriving—alongside blues—in brothels and saloons in the American South. Soon, white musicians got in on the act, forming their own groups. However, the white status quo wouldn't embrace jazz until the swing era or golden age of jazz (1935–1945).

FACT

Jazz might have remained a regional phenomenon if it wasn't for a boom in the recording industry and a migration of New Orleans jazz musicians, including Louis Armstrong, to cities like Chicago and New York. It was in these urban settings that hot jazz truly took shape.

By 1935, swing captivated audiences throughout the world, due in large part to the popularity of the radio. During this period, big bands lead by Tommy Dorsey, Benny Goodman, Count Basie, Chick Webb, Duke Ellington, and others ruled the airwaves.

However, by 1946 the swing era was in decline, and by the mid-1950s America's youth had traded swing altogether for rock-and-roll.

In the late 1940s, a subgenre of jazz emerged called bebop. This largely cerebral style of music allowed bassists to develop as soloists. However, the electric bass wouldn't be integrated into jazz until the mid to late 1960s. Throughout the 1970s, artists began experimenting with a jazz hybrid known as "fusion." Fusion mixed jazz harmonies with the power and energy of rock. Fusion artists also used electric instruments including guitars, keyboards, and synthesizers. On bass guitar, Jaco Pastorius epitomized virtuosity on recordings with Weather Report, Pat Metheny, Joni Mitchell, and others. His solo outings are also renowned, especially his self-titled debut *Jaco Pastorius* (1976).

Jaco Pastorius

Jaco Pastorius (1951–1987) is arguably the most important and ground-breaking electric bassist in history. Jaco, as he is known, was an innovator in all aspects of the instrument, and he was famous for playing on a fretless bass. As you might guess, a fretless bass does not have metal frets; therefore, intonation is entirely up to the bassist. Fretless basses also have a distinct tone since fingertips absorb energy and sound differently than metal strips (frets). Fretless basses also approximate the sound of an upright bass because the bassist has the ability to slide into notes using true glissandos or pitch bends.

FIGURE 8–1 illustrates how Jaco generated a groove by using sixteenth notes. As much as Jaco was known for his technical prowess, he was also a master of using space punctuated by syncopated, funky riffs.

The work of Jaco Pastorius continues to inspire many electric bassists. Jaco's innovations will also serve as a vehicle for your development throughout this book. You'll be encountering more and more difficult issues in bass performance as you work your way through this book. As they arise, you will, in a sense, automatically learn more about the brilliant artistry of Jaco.

FIGURE 8–1. Jaco sixteenths

TRACK 14

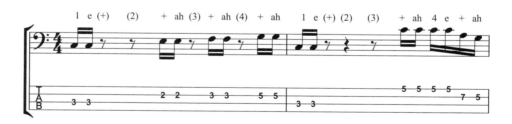

Be mindful when counting these rhythms!

The Shuffle

Blues and jazz wouldn't be the same without swing. As Duke Ellington said, "It don't mean a thing if it ain't got that swing." But in order to get a handle on what swing is, you need to understand the rhythms that inform it.

True swing is not necessarily an exact form of rhythmic subdivision. There is a point in analyzing rhythm where, as in many areas of musical theory, precise mathematical relationships break down. This is the place in music where the human element has the final say! When it comes to swing, having a feel for it may be something you instinctively have or don't have.

But rest assured, swing—as elusive as it may be—can be wrestled down to earth. In short, swing can be reduced down to a series of eighth-note triplets and triplet rests.

Eighth-note triplets can be thought of as a three-part subdivision of a quarter note. In other words, each beat is split into three equal parts. By saying the word "triplet" in time with your beat, you can approximate this rhythm: "tri-puh-let, tri-puh-let, tri-puh-let, tri-puh-let."

In order to get more comfortable with triplets, take a look at the rhythmic pattern used in **FIGURE 8–2**. Tap it out with one hand while the other hand (or your foot) taps out the pulse. Make sure to keep both the beat and the triplets completely steady and even. The first note of each triplet group should line up exactly with the quarter-note pulse, which is shown on the bottom of the staff. Also, notice the method used to count the triplets: "1-trip-let, 2-trip-let, 3-trip-let, 4-trip-let." This is the most effective way to count triplets since it uses numbers to elucidate the beat.

Now you are ready to check out a swing feel derived from triplets. **FIGURE 8–3** brings you back to the bass and playing swing triplets on G. First tap this pattern, and then apply the rhythm to the bass. You'll notice that this figure is the same as **FIGURE 8–2** except that an eighth rest replaces the middle triplet in each beat. In other words, an eighth rest replaces the "trip" in the count.

FIGURE 8–2.
Eighth-note
triplets with a
quarter-note
pulse

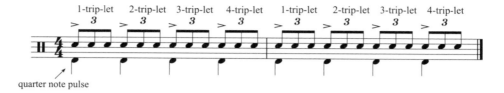

FIGURE 8–3.
Swing triplets

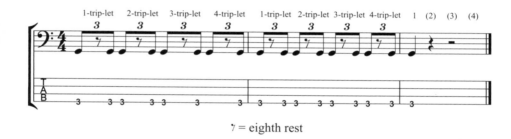

♪ = eighth rest

If you repeat the figure over and over again and listen carefully, you'll start to get the feel of swing. In order to do this, you must always remain relaxed. Tension or stiffness kills swing! This swing feel in **FIGURE 8–3** is also referred to as a shuffle, especially when this rhythm is emphasized in the bass line and rhythm section (as in blues music).

When swing first developed, it was less formal. The rhythmic figures you have used to play swing are close approximations. Oddly enough, the usual way to notate swing is to not really to notate it at all. Rather, swing is generally written as eighth notes with the word "swing" written above the notation. This is done as musical shorthand. It's also easier on the eyes to read eighth notes rather than triplets.

FIGURE 8–4 has a shuffle bass groove written first as triplets then as eighth notes. When you play the eighth notes, be sure to interpret them as "swing eighths" or triplets. **FIGURE 8–4** compares the two types of notation. From now on, swing rhythms will always be written with eighth notes. Also, the word "swing" will always be indicated above the notation in the figure.

FIGURE 8–4. Triplets and swing eighths

TRACK 15

In Figure 8-4, measures 1 and 2 *sound the same* as measure 3 and 4.

When you play swing eighths, eighth notes are interpreted like triplets →

Two-Beat Bass Lines

One type of bass pattern that is used in blues and jazz is the two-beat bass line. You've actually encountered it before with previous bass figures that used the movement from root to fifth on beats one and three. That is one version of the two-beat feel. A two-beat bass line can use other notes and rhythms as long as beats one and three are emphasized and beats two and four are left more or less empty. Also, a swing feel may be incorporated through the use of skip notes that directly precede beats one and three. Through variation and randomization you can make a simple two-beat line more attention grabbing.

FIGURE 8–5 provides a two-beat swing line. In the first four measures you will play the two-beat line straight without skip-note ornamentation. For the last four measures you'll play the same bass line but with skip notes added. This type of two-beat groove is often used to give a restrained feel to a jazzy song. It may also be used to give the song a bouncy, carefree feel.

FIGURE 8–5.

Two-beat swing

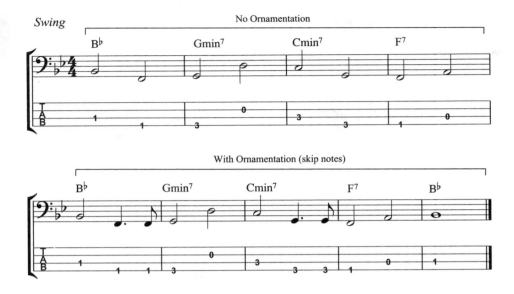

Often, two-beat bass lines will be used at the beginning or head of a slow jazz tune. After playing the head, the bass and rhythm section may decide to escalate the intensity of the music by switching to a heavier swing feel such as a shuffle or a walking bass line.

QUESTION?

In jazz, what is the "head"?

The term "head" refers to the melody of a jazz tune. Usually the head is played at the beginning and at the end of a song. After the head is played, soloists take their turn improvising over the chord changes. Once the soloing is complete, it's customary to play the head once again before bringing the tune to a close.

Since jazz and blues are highly improvisatory, you will need to come up with bass lines on the fly. You will also need to use listening skills to decide what type of bass part (shuffle, two-beat, walking) is most appropriate. You may be able to experiment with these possibilities at a jam session or some other less formal musical setting where improvisation, spontaneity, and experimentation are normal and, in fact, expected.

Walking Bass Lines

Walking bass patterns are among the most common (and essential) musical devices employed by blues and jazz bassists. The basic goal of a walking bass line is to help join two consecutive chords through a logical, melodic path. In other words, walking bass lines are used to bridge the gap between neighboring chords. There is no one right way to do this; however, there are usually some obvious choices to pick from.

The most common type of rhythm used in walking bass lines is the quarter note. If a chord shifts every measure in 4/4 time, you will have three quarter-note slots or gaps to fill in after you play each root note. This approach assumes that you are playing the root of each chord on beat one. Beats two, three, and four are then left for walking. **FIGURE 8–6** outlines this approach.

FIGURE 8–6.
Constructing a walking bass line

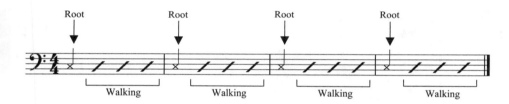

QUESTION?

What are the choices for filling in walking bass lines?
When filling in the open slots between roots, you can use scales, arpeggios (chord tones), or chromatics, which are passing tones that move in half steps. You also may use a combination of all of the above, which is the most common approach used by bassists.

Chapters 14 and 16 provide a more detailed account of how to create bass lines with chromatics or passing tones. For now, you should explore scales and arpeggios.

FIGURE 8–7 has you filling in the gaps using arpeggios and scales. For this exercise you'll be playing what is known as a ii–V–I chord progression. This is a common type of progression used over and over again in jazz. The first two times through the ii–V–I chord changes you'll be using arpeggios or notes extracted from the chord. On the third and fourth pass, you'll be using a more scalar approach, which builds off of the chord and the diatonic key center. In other words, you'll be using the scale of the key (the I chord), but you will be basing its upward or downward movement on the root of each chord (the ii, V, or I chords). When this is fully realized, it is called a mode. In **FIGURE 8–7** you don't have time to play the whole mode (octave to octave), but you will be using notes culled from modes. Chapter 11 explores modes in greater detail.

FIGURE 8–7. Walking with arpeggios and scales

TRACK 16

Getting back to the roots of jazz, it's time to learn the basic structure of the blues form. The best way to learn this form is to use chord functions or Roman numerals. Contrary to most of the rules of classical, Western harmony, the blues uses a dominant seventh on all of its chords. This is why early blues and jazz was so revolutionary (and what helps to keep it so relevant and powerful even today). Although there are many variations on the blues form, **FIGURE 8–8** shows you the basic twelve-bar structure.

FIGURE 8–8.
Basic blues form

FIGURE 8–9.
Blues with walking bass line

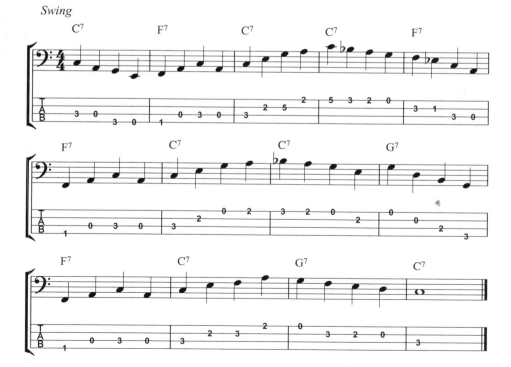

Now it's time to use a walking bass line in the blues. **FIGURE 8–9** makes use of sixths and dominant seventh harmonic extensions. You'll again be integrating scales and arpeggios with the goal of creating compelling musical statements. Once you've mastered the bass line in **FIGURE 8–9**, practice filling in beats two, three, and four with your own walking bass variations.

Pedal Tones, Ostinatos, and Harmonics

Although two-beat and walking bass lines are preeminent in jazz and blues, there are some other, somewhat miscellaneous, techniques that can be inventive, refreshing, and downright fun. Not surprisingly, Jaco Pastorius was known for employing all of these in creative ways.

The first item to check out is the use of pedal tones. A pedal tone, or "pedal" for short, couldn't be easier to play since it's just one note! The whole idea of a pedal is to plant one good, solid bass note underneath shifting chords on top. A pedal's power comes from the fact that it is stationary. The pedal immediately grabs the listener's attention by building harmonic tension and emotional intensity. Also, a pedal often differs from the root of the chord. This further dramatizes the pedal's tension and release. **FIGURE 8–10** illustrates the use of pedal tones on another, more advanced, blues form.

Sometimes it can be positively hypnotic to hear compelling melodic idea repeated over and over again. The musical term for this is *ostinato*. When an ostinato is played as a bass line, it can have this same, almost intoxicating, effect. A great example of this is the bass part on the Miles Davis classic "All Blues" as played by the great Paul Chambers. **FIGURE 8–11** is an ostinato that simulates Chambers's bass part. Again, you will see another slight modification to the blues form. Also, you're playing in 3/4 time on this example.

One of Jaco Pastorius's most innovative techniques was his use of harmonic overtones. His technique was so advanced that it goes well beyond the scope of this book. However, you should get a chance to try harmonics.

To achieve this special sound, you need to rest your middle finger on any string over frets twelve, seven, or five. There are more locations where harmonics can be achieved, and you should have fun trying to discover them, but it's easiest to achieve harmonics on one of the above mentioned frets.

FIGURE 8–10. Pedal tones

TRACK 17

In measures eleven and twelve, the chords change but you pedal on an E.

To play a harmonic, gently rest your fingertip exactly over the metal fret. This is the sweet spot for playing a harmonic. Be sure not to press all the way down to the neck. Once your left hand is in position, pluck with your right hand. A fraction of a second later, nearly simultaneously with your plucking, remove your left-hand finger from the string. Listen for a ringing, almost bell-like, tone. You may not hear it at first, but once you practice this it should become easier to achieve. Through experimentation you can mix different harmonics to create melodic patterns and even chords that have their own distinctive sound. If you choose, you can also tune your bass by using harmonics. **FIGURE 8–12** gives you a chance to use harmonics.

FIGURE 8–11.

Ostinato bass line

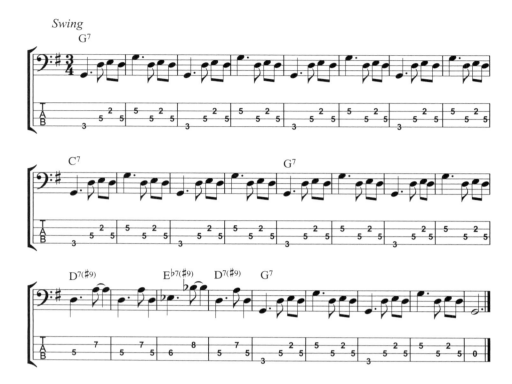

FIGURE 8–12. Using harmonics

TRACK 18

Play all notes as harmonics and let each note ring out.
8va means to play an octave higher than written.

Chapter 9
R & B, Soul, Motown, and Funk

R & B, soul, Motown, and funk are all related terms, and indeed, related idioms. In fact, in some situations these terms might even be interchangeable. However, rhythm and blues (R & B) should be regarded as the parent company to soul, Motown, and funk. In this chapter you will begin to learn about the bass lines, techniques, and theory that inform these styles. This includes slap bass and hammer-on techniques, walking bass lines, and funk riffs using pentatonics.

A Brief History of R & B

R & B is a general term used to describe the pop music of black America. R & B dates back to around 1930, and it is still being performed today. In addition to the obvious influence of the blues, early R & B contained elements of gospel and folk. It also culled from the syncopated rhythms of jazz.

The term *R & B* was invented by Jerry Wexler and *Billboard* magazine in the late 1940s. It was seen as a softer description for what was previously known as "race records." For all intents and purposes, Atlantic Records, in the late 1940s and 1950s, was the first record label to advertise music as "rhythm and blues." In fact, R & B's popularity is due in large part to the marketing strategies of Turkish-born record executives Ahmet and Nasuhi Ertegun.

QUESTION?

What does the term *R & B* really mean?
R & B is a catchall phrase used by record companies to label popular music by black artists. Since the 1960s, subgenres of R & B have become more prevalent as record companies seek to market musical styles like brand names. One such brand name is contemporary R & B. This style of music differs greatly from the music Jerry Wexler wrote about in the 1940s.

Although it's hard to pinpoint R & B's humble beginnings, it emerged after the blues migrated north. This occurred after both world wars. R & B's predecessors, or arguably its earliest practitioners, were urban jump-blues stylists Louis Jordan, Big Joe Turner, and others. In the 1950s, black musicians of various backgrounds found success under the R & B umbrella. Early luminaries included Ruth Brown, Bobby Bland, and the so-called father of R & B, Ray Charles. In reality, Ray Charles was hardly the originator of R & B. However, he was R & B's most visible figure in the 1950s and 1960s.

It's not always easy to tell the difference between R & B and its stylistic cousins, forerunners, and offshoots. For example, Ray Charles made forays into jazz, country and western, and mainstream pop. Dinah Washington was a distinguished jazz singer and R & B artist. Hank Ballard (composer of the song "The Twist") was arguably an early rock-and-roll singer. When you listen to these and other R & B artists, you will hear a potpourri of musical styles. Despite this, traditional R & B usually contains the following elements:

- Bluesy melodies and improvisation
- Passionate, preacher-like vocal performances
- Use of a backbeat (snare drum strikes on beats two and four)
- Tightly synchronized bass and drums (On bass, early patterns were four-beat walking lines. Later, eighth-note grooves and syncopated sixteenth-note patterns were employed. The drummer typically mimicked bass patterns on his kick drum.)
- Timbral variety (You might hear a smooth-toned singer followed by a growling saxophone.)
- The use of a twelve-bar blues form (not an ironclad rule)

Soul, Motown, and Funk

Originally, soul was a conscious return to R & B's gospel roots. Soul gradually turned secular as black crooners Otis Redding, Sam Cooke, and Marvin Gaye wrote songs that preached messages of love and worship without specific reference to God or Christ. Aretha Franklin was also a key figure in soul's secular development even though she was heavily influenced by gospel legend Mahalia Jackson. James Brown was another towering figure in soul music. In time, he would be called the Godfather of Soul.

Motown is a type of soul music that originated from Detroit, Michigan, which was known as "Motor City" or Mo-town for short. Female singing groups such as the Supremes and the Marvelettes dominated early Motown, and on bass, James Jamerson (1936–1983) pioneered a whole new style of playing. His punchy, deep-pocketed grooves (plucked mostly with the index finger) have influenced generations of R & B, funk, soul, and rock bassists.

Jamerson played memorable bass lines on songs such as "I Heard It Through the Grapevine" by Gladys Knight and the Pips, "You Can't Hurry Love" by the Supremes, "My Girl" by the Temptations, "For Once in My Life" by Stevie Wonder, and dozens of other hits. However, Jamerson wouldn't get the recognition he deserved until he was posthumously inducted into the Rock and Roll Hall of Fame in 2000. Virtually all of the bass lines you will learn in this chapter have some connection to Jamerson and his innovations.

Funk is a broad musical category. Virtually any music—from Miles Davis to the Average White Band—could be labeled funk. For many listeners, James Brown was funk's greatest ambassador. He scored big with hits such as "I Got You (I Feel Good)," "Papa's Got a Brand New Bag," and "Sex Machine."

Another significant funk group was Parliament Funkadelic, the originators of the popular P-Funk sound. Led by George Clinton, Parliament Funkadelic's style was greatly enhanced by the sleek, adventurous bass playing of Bootsy Collins. Collins was one of the first bassists to use the Mu-Tron envelope filter (synthesizer sound effect) on his bass. He also used a unique slap bass technique that included whole-hand slaps on the bass. Humorously, Collins likened this slap technique to spanking a baby's bottom. You will learn more about slap techniques later in the chapter.

R & B Bass Lines

R & B bass lines have a lineage that passes through many genres, including blues, folk, ragtime, boogie-woogie, Dixieland, swing, and even marching band music. R & B bass parts borrow generously from those developed on piano, upright bass, and tuba. However, with the advent of the electric bass, and electronic music in general, the bass has also grown more modern and cutting edge.

Before funk and rock existed, R & B bass was closely related to blues itself. At that time, bass lines were typically centered around the root of the chord, usually played on beat one. This was followed by thirds, fifths, sixths, dominant sevenths, and even seconds on beats two through four. The walking bass line (with the quarter-note pulse) comprised the basic rhythmical feel in old-school R & B. This type of bass line also inspired much of early rock-and-roll, which, for all intents and purposes, was merely a hyped-up form of R & B. **FIGURE 9–1** illustrates a typical pattern that might be used.

FIGURE 9–1.
R & B walking
bass line

The major pentatonic scale is the basis for a wide variety of bass lines. Composed of five different notes (the prefix "penta" means five), the major pentatonic is used extensively in contemporary pop, R & B, funk, soul, and other styles. Its origin, however, is extremely primitive. Many ancient and ethnic forms of music use the pentatonic scale (as does blues) as the basis for the melody and is one of the most universal scales of all time.

There are two main types of pentatonic scales: major and minor. Each major pentatonic has a relative minor. The relative minor pentatonic contains the same notes as its major counterpart. Relative minor pentatonics are found a minor third below (or a major sixth above) the given major pentatonic.

The most common type of major pentatonic uses a tonic, a major second, a major third, a perfect fifth, and a major sixth. You should familiarize yourself with all the possible positions and configurations for this scale.

You will learn more about minor pentatonics later on in this chapter. For now, **FIGURE 9–2** shows you three typical positions for A major pentatonic. All three examples use a closed position. This simply means that there are no open strings. Closed position is beneficial because it is moveable up and down the fretboard. In **FIGURE 9–2**, the first and last notes are tonic pitches. If chord changes were present, the tonic would correlate to the root of the chord (in this case, A).

The major pentatonic can typically be used on any major chord in R & B. In order to compose a bass line, notes are often pulled from this scale, sometimes in some combination with other scales or musical devices. Every time the chord shifts, the corresponding major pentatonic may shift too. **FIGURE 9–3** shows how you can use three pieces of three major pentatonic scales. On each chord, the pentatonic shifts to correspond with the chord. You should try composing (or improvising) your own bass lines using these three scales. In order to do this, play the root of each scale on beat one and a segment of the appropriate scale on beats two, three, and four. This assumes you're playing in 4/4 time.

In Chapter 7 you learned that the dominant seventh interval—technically called a minor seventh—is a special chord extension. Harmonically, it captures the essence of the blues like no other extension. As you can imagine, the dominant seventh is also an essential element in R & B. When you combine the dominant seventh with the major pentatonic, you have even more good options. Some of these options are shown in **FIGURE 9–4**. Here you will play the same chord changes as **FIGURE 9–3** but with a new bass line; the bass line used in **FIGURE 9–4** always incorporates the dominant seventh.

FIGURE 9–2.
A Major
pentatonic in
three positions

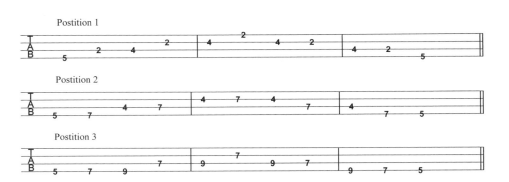

FIGURE 9–3.
Major pentatonics
on three chords

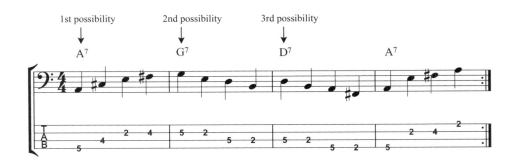

FIGURE 9–4.
Expanding
your use
of major
pentatonics

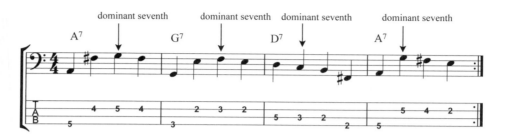

Funky Bass Lines

Now that you have some experience with basic R & B bass lines, it's time to take the leap into funk music. Once R & B emerged from the blues and began to take on a life of its own, R & B gradually began to get a little funkier. R & B bass originally relied on grooves such as swing and shuffle. These styles employed more of a walking bass line. But as R & B evolved away from these grooves, bassists began to play more sophisticated rhythms.

In essence, the quarter-note walking bass line was now spiced up with more notes and more rhythmic variety. However, most funk uses the same note content as early R & B. **FIGURE 9–5** uses the same chord changes and scales from **FIGURES 9–3** and **9–4**; however, you will ornament them rhythmically, or funk them up. Play the eighth notes in this figure straight. In other words, do not give them a swing or triplet feel.

There has to be some other harmonic material that bassists use to enliven the music. An interesting addition to the basic framework is chromatics. Remember, chromatics refer to half steps or semitones on the fretted electric bass. (Upright basses do not have frets so they can subdivide

FIGURE 9–5. Three chords funked up

TRACK 19

pitch almost infinitely. The same is true of fretless bass guitars.) On your instrument, a chromatic means that you will move up or down the frets in a consecutive manner. In other words, you will not skip any frets in your movement along the fretboard.

Chromatics are used to connect chord tones and scale degrees. A common place to see chromatic movement is in between the third and fifth scale degrees or the sixth and the eighth (octave) scale degrees. This is assuming that you're working off of a major pentatonic. Also, inserting a small chromatic passage between the second and major third scale degrees is common. In reality, you can use chromatics any way you see fit as long as it sounds right. Check out some chromatic ideas in **FIGURE 9–6**.

FIGURE 9–6. Using chromatics

TRACK 20

Be careful of the syncopated rhythms!

Minor Pentatonic Scales

Another fixture of funky bass playing is the minor pentatonic scale. Related to the major pentatonic, the minor pentatonic uses the same notes as its related major except that they are framed differently. In other words, they have an alternate tonic or home base. **FIGURE 9–7** compares two positions of related major and minor pentatonic scales. Play these and listen to how the same basic content is subtly changed by emphasizing a different tonic pitch.

FIGURE 9–7.

Relative major and minor pentatonic scales

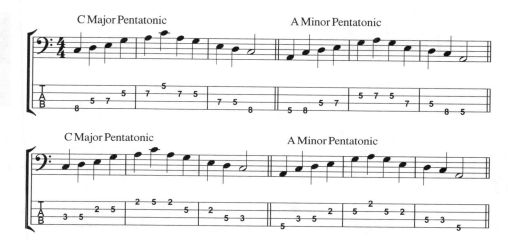

As you can see, the positioning in **FIGURE 9–7** is basically the same as the major pentatonic position you learned earlier in the chapter. By learning all of the different positions for major and minor pentatonics, you are essentially learning both the major and minor pentatonic scales simultaneously—a definite bonus! Learn all of the positions for major and minor pentatonics on the fretboard because you will want to use them in real musical situations.

Bear in mind that the minor pentatonic is used sparingly in R & B and its offshoots. It most commonly appears as an ostinato or repeated riff. It is also great for improvising and soloing. (You'll explore soloing in Chapter 11.) Often the minor pentatonic is used in minor keys on the i chord. It can also be employed on major chords such as I7 or V7 when you want to give the music a bluesy feel. Admittedly, the minor pentatonic's usage is subject to taste on any given chord, but the novice bassist tends to overuse it.

In **FIGURE 9–8**, you'll see a minor pentatonic used on an A7 (dominant seventh) chord. For the second dominant seventh chord (D7), you will use a major pentatonic with a chromatic passage added in. This figure shows you how to mix major and minor pentatonics within a musical phrase.

FIGURE 9-8. Using major and minor pentatonics

TRACK 21

How do I know when to use the minor pentatonic?

Your ear is the best judge. By using your ear, you will eventually be able to tell where minor pentatonics fit and where they don't. If it sounds too harsh or overly bluesy, try the major pentatonic of the chord instead. Be careful when using a minor pentatonic over a major chord. The minor pentatonic uses a flatted third. Technically, this clashes with the major third of the chord.

Slap Bass Lines

One of the newer additions to the bassist's vocabulary is a technique called slapping. This technique is also called thumbing. Not all bassists use this technique; it all comes down to personal style and musical context. Popularized in the 1970s and 1980s, slapping can be heard in the electric bass work of Stanley Clarke, Larry Graham, Flea, Mark King, and Victor Wooten.

The technique of slapping is based on an alternating motion between the thumb and the index finger of the right hand (assuming you're holding the bass right-handed). This technique is very percussive in nature and is used in funk, disco, soul, and fusion jazz to create bass lines and solos.

When slapping, the side of the thumb hits the strings like a mallet. This is called thumbing. Use a rotating motion in your wrist and forearm to strike the string forcefully. The thumb generally attacks the lower strings.

The second half of the technique is snapping on the higher strings. The snap is performed with the index finger of the right hand. Its goal is to pluck in such a fashion so that the strings snap back against the bass guitar. This is accomplished by using the index finger as a hook. First, shape the finger like a hook. Second, position your finger under the string. Third, pluck the string so that it smacks back against the neck and pickups. Both the thumbing and snapping aspects of slap bass need to be practiced quite extensively in order to achieve the funky sound that is the signature of this technique. It's also recommended that you watch a bass player do this in order to better visualize the technique (see Film/DVD in Appendix B).

A great way to get started is to play octaves up and down the neck. When you do this, use the thumbing technique on the low notes. On the high notes, snap the string with your index finger. A common slap bass pattern is illustrated in **FIGURE 9–9**. This bass line also uses chromatics to better connect the two chords.

Another technique that goes hand in hand with slapping is the hammer-on. As you slap, hammer-ons are performed with the left hand by striking the fretboard with your fingers. This means that in between thumbs and snaps you will hammer the string. If you're manipulating two notes with adjacent fingers, the higher finger literally bangs onto the fret so that it produces a new sound. In other words, after a thumb or snap, the higher finger in the left hand hammers the second note. The hammer-on is aided by the fact that there is already extra energy in the string due to the excessive force that thumbing and snapping provide.

FIGURE 9–9. Slapping octaves

TRACK 22

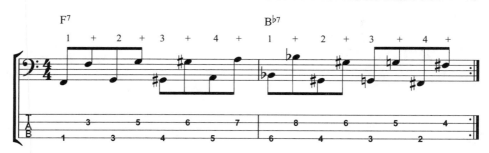

Thumb downbeats (1, 2, 3, 4) and snap upbeats (+).

The whole process can be summarized in three easy steps:

1. Press down a string using fingers one, two, or three in the left hand.
2. Thumb or snap this same string using your right hand.
3. Forcefully hammer-on the string using an adjacent finger in the left hand. The finger you use for hammering lies above the first note's finger. When you do this, a second note is produced. Remember, fingers are numbered one through four—index through pinky—respectively.

The hammer-on technique can also be used minus the thumbing/snapping aspect, but it requires you to apply more energy in the left hand. All in all, a hammer-on may be used in any appropriate passage of notes: fingered, picked, thumbed, or snapped. Generally, hammer-ons help to make musical passages more legato and smooth.

In **FIGURE 9–10**, you'll see a riff based on a minor pentatonic scale. Try thumbing the lower notes while snapping the higher pitched ones. Because the higher notes fall in quick succession, and because the fingering in the left hand makes it possible to hammer, you can easily employ the hammer-on technique in this exercise.

FIGURE 9–10. Slapping with hammer-on

TRACK 23

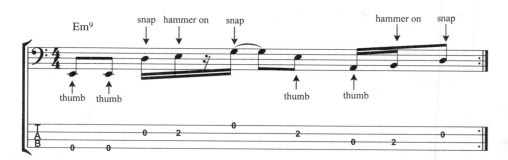

Chapter 10
Latin Styles

In Chapter 10 you will learn about a variety of Latin musical styles. First, you will delve into the history and roots of this music, and then you will learn some common Latin bass lines. Since Latin music comprises so many styles, this chapter focuses on those central to the electric bass. These include the bossa nova, salsa, reggae, ska, calypso, and soca. For additional information on these rich and fascinating musical cultures, be sure to see Appendix B.

A Brief History of Latin Music

By now you know that stylistic labels like "jazz" and "rock" are general terms used to describe a wide variety of genres. "Latin" music is no exception. Like the blues, Latin American styles are best understood through regionalism. Latin music comes from the inhabitants of Mexico, Central and South America, and the Caribbean islands. The islands of Cuba, Puerto Rico, the Dominican Republic, Jamaica, and Trinidad and Tobago are particularly important to Latin's development. Latin also has a large following in the United States. Cities such as Miami, New York, and Los Angeles teem with Latin American culture and music.

Latin music is rooted in Africa, namely the musical cultures of Nigeria, Angola, and the Congo. Moreover, European folk music, especially Spanish music, influenced early Latin styles. More recently, jazz, rock, and Top 40 radio has had an enormous impact on Latin's evolution.

The electric bass is commonly used in Latin hybrids. One of these hybrids is Latin jazz. Latin jazz dates back to the early 1900s. For example, the Argentinean tango was used in a section of W. C. Handy's classic tune "St. Louis Blues." During the 1930s, Duke Ellington, influenced by valve trombonist Juan Tizol, wrote the now famous "Caravan." After World War II, the Latin jazz explosion occurred due in part to Dizzy Gillespie, a bebop trumpeter, who was enchanted by Afro-Cuban music. By the 1950s, Latin big bands led by Tito Puente, Perez Prado, Chico O'Farrill, and Machito sparked many of the trends in dance such as the cha-cha-cha and the mambo that we now consider commonplace. The enchanting Desi Arnaz also helped to expand Latin's appeal through performances by his orchestra on the hit TV show *I Love Lucy*.

Latin's Evolution

In the 1960s, the bossa nova emerged in Brazil. Its most important composer, Antonio Carlos Jobim, combined relaxed samba rhythms with cool jazz. He found the perfect blend in tunes such as "Desafinado" and "One Note Samba," which became pop hits in the United States.

In 1963, Joao Gilberto collaborated with Jobim and jazz saxophonist Stan Getz to record an album entitled *Getz/Gilberto*. The last-minute addition of Gilberto's wife, Astrud, on a tune called "The Girl from Ipanema" proved to be quite significant. Because of Astrud's silky voice, "Ipanema" became a mega hit in the United States and eventually a worldwide classic.

Latin pop is another hybrid that uses the electric bass. This style enjoys a wide fan base thanks to guitarist Carlos Santana and pop singers Gloria Estefan, Marc Anthony, Jon Secada, Ricky Martin, Jennifer Lopez, Selena, Celia Cruz, and Julio and Enrique Iglesias. Meringue rhythms are commonly used in Latin pop. Like most Latin styles, the meringue goes all the way back to the slave trade. Its lively feel—marked by thumping quarter notes— has proven infectious in discotheques across the globe.

In Trinidad, the electric bass is used to accompany steel drum or steelpan groups. Some of these groups use singers; others are strictly instrumental. The colloquial music of Trinidad is written mostly in major keys, and it has a carefree, lilting feel to it. Trinidadian genres that use electric bass include calypso and soca. Interestingly, the most famous calypso artist, Harry Belafonte, is not Trinidadian. Rather, he's a New York City native with Jamaican ancestry.

Jamaica is known largely for reggae music. In this style, the electric bass is almost always used. The etymology of the word "reggae" is in dispute. Some say it was first used formally by Toots and the Maytals on a 1968 single called "Do the Reggae," but others trace its origins back much further. The music itself is very old. Early versions of reggae date all the way back to a tribe called the Regga who lived in West Africa. The most famous reggae artist is the late, great Bob Marley. Marley claimed that the word *reggae* meant "the king's music" in Spanish. Most Jamaican roots reggae artists are also Rastafarians. This religious movement considers Emperor Haile Selassie I of Ethiopia to be a black messiah.

FACT

Reggae is a bouncy style of music that borrows from African rhythms, the blues, American pop, and, more recently, rap music. It stresses upbeats, or "ands," and often uses a loose triplet feel.

American and British pop artists have long incorporated reggae elements in their music. For example, Paul Simon used a reggae feel for his 1972 hit "Mother and Child Reunion." Also, Sting used a reggae groove on several songs, including "Walking on the Moon" and "Love is the Seventh Wave." Further, Bobby McFerrin scored a big hit with his reggae-inspired tune "Don't Worry, Be Happy" in 1988. Additionally, Bonnie Raitt used a reggae feel on her 1989 single "Have a Heart." These are but a few examples of reggae's huge crossover potential.

Ska music is reggae's most important precursor. Like reggae, ska has undergone many changes throughout the decades. Contemporary ska is marked by very fast, energetic performances. Like reggae, the afterbeat, or "and," is stressed in this music. British bands such as the English Beat, the Specials, and Madness epitomized ska's so-called second wave. Ska's third wave combines elements of hardcore rock. The American group the Mighty Mighty Bosstones is probably the best example of this. Their music is often referred to as "ska-core," and their bassist, Joe Gittleman, contributed greatly to their sound.

Brazilian Bass Lines

Brazilian music, like all subgenres of Latin music, is far too vast to be reduced down to one or two patterns. But you have to start somewhere! Probably the best place to start is the famous bossa nova, which is a gentler, romantic variation of the samba. The bossa nova comes from Rio de Janeiro, a city in southeastern Brazil. It is a gentle, medium-tempo groove that is as cool as an ocean breeze. Antonio Carlos Jobim's catalog of standards has become the template for most tunes in the bossa nova style.

FACT

Samba is a ritualistic style of music and dance. Community groups called "escolas de samba," or samba schools, keep the samba tradition alive through their annual performances at Carnaval. Carnaval is a colorful, often rowdy, festival that attracts thousands to parade grounds each year.

Most bassists approach a bossa (as it is often known for short) with the standard root-and-fifth approach. Hopefully by now you're noticing that this pattern is universal in bass playing. In Brazilian music, the groove is what sets this pattern apart from other root-and-fifth styles. Interestingly, many of Jobim's actual recordings use more of a root-to-root approach, which is even simpler than what most bassists would do today. Nevertheless, **FIGURE 10–1** shows the typical rhythmic motif used by modern bossa nova bassists. This simple but elegant bass line was also made famous in the Steely Dan hit "Ricky Don't Lose that Number" (*Pretzel Logic*, 1974).

FIGURE 10–1.
Basic bossa nova

The bossa nova has a light, airy feel!

ALERT!

Bossa nova, like almost all other types of Latin music, uses straight eighths. This means it uses nonswing eighth notes. In a fundamental sense, the straight-eighth feel is what separates a Latin bossa from a typical midtempo jazz tune. They are almost opposite grooves. Bossa novas tend to use jazz harmonies, so it's common for jazz players to sprinkle bossa novas in between standard swing tunes.

As previously stated, the bossa nova is highly influenced, in a harmonic sense, by jazz. A chord used in both styles is the half diminished, or the minor seventh flat five chord. When you use the minor ii–V–I progression in Chapter 17, you'll delve more into the theory behind this type of chord. For now, just remember that this chord is used as a ii chord in a minor key. Also, when this chord appears in music, you *must* flat the fifth in the root/fifth pattern. In **FIGURE 10–2**, the common bossa nova bass pattern is written with flatted fifths. The arpeggio for the chord is also given to you so that you can learn the true outline of the notes that comprise it.

Now try mixing up the chords using minor seventh flat five chords and other harmonic extensions. In **FIGURE 10–3**, some of the fifths are played below the root. Technically, this creates a perfect fourth interval between the two pitches. (See measures four and six.) Given the role of the root, you should still think of the lower pitch as a fifth.

FIGURE 10–2.

Using the half diminished or minor seventh flat five chord

This pattern uses flatted fifths or tritones!

FIGURE 10–3.

Bossa nova chord variations

Afro-Cuban Grooves

The music of Cuba is particularly vital to Latin music. Afro-Cuban music is also known as salsa music. As stated earlier, there are very many versions of salsa. Subgenres include son, rumba, mambo, timba, charanga, and others. Some of these are not significantly different from the bossa nova except that they are usually played a lot faster and with some additional rhythmical variation. For the purposes of this book, you will learn some generalized patterns that can be used in Afro-Cuban contexts. **FIGURE 10–4** is one such example. Notice that the rhythm is similar to the basic bossa nova pattern used in **FIGURE 10–1**.

FIGURE 10–4.
Up-tempo
root-and-fifth
salsa variation

What if the chord is minor or major? Do I do something different?
As long as you ignore or stay away from the third of the chord, which is standard practice in a root/fifth pattern anyway, you can play the same bass lines over a major or minor chord. In other words, the root/fifth pattern works equally for both.

In many cases, syncopation is used to further spice things up in Latin music. A common device is to use two dotted quarter notes and then a regular quarter note to give an off-the-beat feel. This may be the more Afro part of the Afro-Cuban feel as it is common for these kinds of rhythms to appear in West African music too. This rhythm is shown in **FIGURE 10–5**. Again, roots and fifths are used.

FIGURE 10–5.
Afro-Cuban groove

Variety is certainly the spice of life, and you'd expect nothing else from something called salsa. A good way to bring in some additional colors is to vary the note order or choices. In **FIGURE 10–6**, you'll use a dominant seventh instead of the octave of the root. This works well on minor seventh chords or major chords with a dominant seventh, often just referred to as dominant seventh chords.

FIGURE 10–6.
Afro-Cuban groove with dominant sevenths

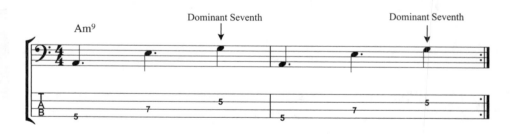

Another common variation is to double up on the fifth by placing it above and below the root. In **FIGURE 10–7**, the fifth replaces the octave. If you want to be creative, you could also create a pattern that alternates between the fifth and octave in each measure.

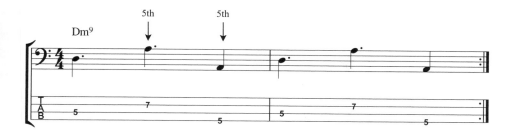

FIGURE 10–7.
Afro-Cuban groove with doubled fifth

Reggae and Ska

Another grand dame of the Caribbean is the island of Jamaica where you'll find reggae as the dominant form of music. In reggae, the bass takes on a slightly more melodic emphasis, although the rhythmical aspects are still just as valued. This is due to the fact that reggae is generally slower and more laid-back than salsa.

Traditional reggae, by the likes of Bob Marley and Peter Tosh, often use bass lines that emphasize arpeggiation. However, there are some rather noteworthy differences between reggae and most other forms of Latin music. For example, the root/fifth bass figure (which itself is a type of arpeggio) and its variations are usually avoided in reggae. Instead, other broken chord patterns are employed. Additionally, rhythms using a potpourri of rests and different note values further enhance the rhythmic and melodic possibilities. In other words, creativity and variation can yield all sorts of interesting results. **FIGURE 10–8** shows one example of this.

Another, somewhat radical, departure from standard bass player practice (in virtually all genres of music) is the omission of beat one. Usually this would be a musical sin for a bassist, but in reggae it is often welcome! Combining this peculiarity with information you already learned, try playing **FIGURE 10–9**. Resting on beat one is sometimes called "dropping the one" or "drop-one."

FIGURE 10–8.
Reggae arpeggios on a standard chord progression

FIGURE 10–9.

Reggae arpeggios with drop-one

In each measure beat *one* is a rest!

One rhythm used constantly in reggae and salsa is the quarter-note triplet. Like the eighth-note triplet that you encountered in Chapter 8, the quarter-note triplet may be an uncomfortable note division. However, with a little practice you'll soon learn how to feel it. Quarter-note triplets create a three-against-two polyrhythm. A polyrhythm superimposes two independent, and seemingly clashing, rhythms on top of one another. In 4/4, the three-against-two polyrhythm is created when you layer three quarter-note triplets over two quarter notes. If this pattern is spread out over one full measure, you will see six quarter-note triplets sitting on top of four quarter notes. **FIGURE 10–10** shows what this looks like.

FIGURE 10–10.

Quarter-note triplet pattern

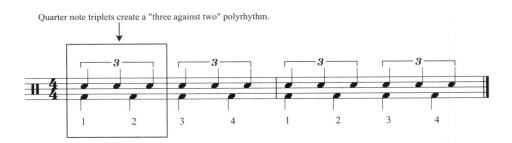

Quarter note triplets create a "three against two" polyrhythm.

Utilizing quarter-note triplets in a bass line is the fun part. Instead of playing standard quarter notes, you can now divide them using triplets. **FIGURE 10–11** brings this unique rhythm to life in a reggae context.

One of the final ingredients in reggae bass lines is space. By purposefully leaving holes in the bass line, suspense is created, and this makes this type of bass line funky. **FIGURE 10–12** shows you how to use space in reggae. If you want to hear how the masters of reggae bass do this, make sure to check out records by Bob Marely and Peter Tosh where you will hear the brilliant work of Aston Barrett and Robbie Shakespeare.

FIGURE 10–11.
Reggae bass
line with
quarter-note
triplets

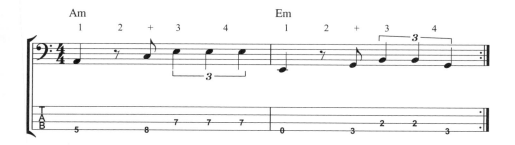

Ska is a style of music that is related to reggae. Ska tends to have a much faster tempo, especially today's hardcore-influenced third wave led by bands the Mighty Mighty Bosstones and No Doubt. The latter features Tony Kanal on electric bass. Ska's first wave actually predates reggae. It also helped to spawn it. During the second wave, ska was popular in the United Kingdom due to the Specials, Madness, and even the Police with Sting on bass.

During their early period, the Police combined ska with punk, creating a style all their own. **FIGURE 10–13** simulates a bass line that Sting might have played with the Police. Notice the use of reggae and ska rhythmical devices.

FIGURE 10–12. Reggae bass—putting it all together

TRACK 24

FIGURE 10–13. Second-wave ska

TRACK 25

Calypso and Soca

Calypso is one of the more ubiquitous styles of Caribbean music. It has waned in fashion as newer and more modern styles have emerged; however, it is still the backbone of many Caribbean styles. Calypso bass lines are characterized by the use of ordered triads and, once again, root/fifth movements. Calypso rhythms often parallel those used in Afro-Cuban music (see **FIGURES 10–5** through **10–7**). However, in calypso the emphasis is on the triad as opposed to unadorned roots and fifths. The use of triads also gives calypso a gentle, often happy, vibe. **FIGURE 10–14** illustrates the simple charm of calypso. It ends with what is known as a "cha, cha, cha" ending. This is a common cliché used in many types of Caribbean music.

FIGURE 10–14. A calypso groove

TRACK 26

A modern variation of calypso is soca. The term is derived from the combination of the words "soul" and "calypso." Soca has been around for decades but had not become well known internationally until the release of the popular single "Hot, Hot, Hot" (as recorded by Buster Poindexter). More recently, the song "Who Let the Dogs Out" (as recorded by the Baha Men) falls under the same musical umbrella.

Soca uses a mix of traditional Caribbean flavors and electronic dance music. As such, it is almost impossible to say exactly what constitutes a traditional soca bass line, though most of them are played in 2/2 time. Nevertheless, **FIGURE 10–15** shows you a modern soca pattern that mimics the main rhythmical motif of "Who Let the Dogs Out." Here there is a strong emphasis on the off beat, which is a salient characteristic of all soca.

There is a lot of cross-pollination between Latin styles. In other words, Latin styles have often influenced one another. Moreover, they continue to change and evolve as new styles of music emerge. In the spirit of the music, you should try to be creative with all forms of Latin music. **FIGURE 10–16** shows a soca improvisation that challenges your ability to play off the beat. Try composing your own Latin-style bass lines that use offbeats. To get inspired, listen to the music of Latin's chief innovators (see Appendix A).

FIGURE 10–15. "Who Let the Dogs Out" groove

TRACK 27

FIGURE 10–16. Soca improvisations

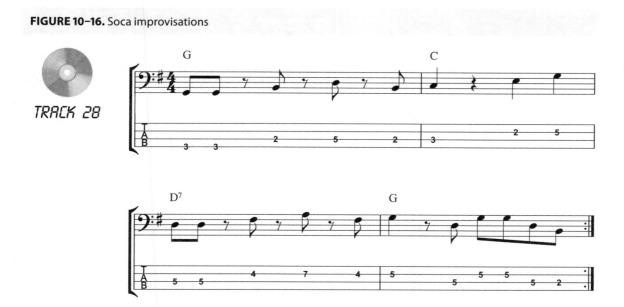

TRACK 28

11

Chapter 11

Soloing Skills

This chapter will introduce you to improvisation, and many of the subsequent chapters will build upon the information presented here. As a primer for soloing, you will first learn about the theory that informs it. You will then begin to apply music theory to licks, riffs, and eventually to a twelve-bar blues. You will notice that the term "motif" is used to describe many of the improvisational snippets found here. This is because solos are often based on symmetrical kernels of ideas from which you create a solo. Often this involves some use of theme and variation.

What Is a Solo?

Soloing is not easy. It requires a thorough command of your instrument and a lot of grace under pressure. Sure, guitarists take the majority of solos in a rock band. But more and more, bass players are showing that they have what it takes when the spotlight is turned on them.

But what is a solo and where do you begin? In order to separate a bass line from a solo, you need to use a different set of musical devices or tools. As you now know, it's routine to construct a bass line using arpeggios or pieces of broken chords. However, when soloing, it provides great contrast to switch to a more scalar or modal approach.

Each specific genre has distinct scales or modes that work in a solo. These scales distinguish style X from style Y. Bear in mind that there could be some cross-pollination since styles of music tend to mix and overlap.

Despite this, in a blues solo your primary tools are pentatonic and blues scales, which you will learn about later in the chapter. In jazz, on the other hand, there is greater emphasis put on using a wide variety of scales. These include diatonic modes, pentatonic scales, diminished scales, chromatic scales, and melodic minor scales. In some styles, you can stick to one or two scales, or perhaps a few scales, that fit with all the chords in the progression. In other genres, you may need to use dozens of scales, each one switching according to each chord's movement. Generally, rock, blues, and other less harmonically sophisticated forms of music require less complicated scalar and modal approaches. In forms like jazz and some types of Latin music, you have to be a master at modulating so that your scales match up with the movement of each chord. That's a tall order indeed, especially when playing in real time.

Using Scales and Modes

In order to pull off a convincing solo, you need to draw melodic inspiration from someplace. The question is where. Scales and modes are the central players in this musical drama. Not only do scales and modes provide the content that you need to cull from, they also help you navigate through the chord progression without playing wrong notes. Without using scales or modes, it'd be practically impossible to play a convincing solo in virtually any musical genre.

Modes are just another type of scale. They appear different from major and minor scales since they are built on different intervallic models. Most traditional modes are just inversions of the common major scale. In other words, modes are formally different from scales but they are constitutively the same.

The essential modes are really just different configurations of the major scale. In fact, they can be constructed out of the major scale, and they are best learned in relationship to it. **FIGURE 11–1** shows all the standard modes related to the C-major scale. Notice the use of Greek names for the modes. The Greeks were among the first to investigate the musical and emotional possibilities of modes. The Greeks named the seven modes after geographic regions or districts in Greece. Pythagoras and his followers were among the first to develop and catalog these modes.

FIGURE 11–1.
Seven modes in relation to C major

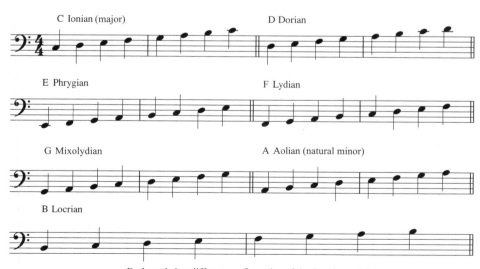

Each mode is a different configuration of the C major scale!

You'll investigate some of these modes on the following pages. When you do, you'll want to practice them in two ways. First, play them using a single position of the major scale. Then play the modes in movable closed positions, which are relative to the tonic of each scale. **FIGURES 11–2** and **11–3** show you what these approaches are like respectively. After you've mastered these figures, use movable closed positions to play the remaining five modes.

FIGURE 11–2.
C Ionian and
D Dorian in
one position

FIGURE 11–3.
C Ionian and
D Dorian
in different
positions

If you wish, you may shift octaves.

Motifs, Repetition, and Rhythmical Variety

Once you get comfortable with scales and modes, you need to push the envelope by using variation and repetition—both melodic and rhythmic. When you are soloing, you should use musical symmetry to make your solo sound coherent and logical. What is musical symmetry? Musical phrases sound symmetrical when they reflect or mirror back on themselves. This means using repetition, both rhythmical and melodic, in your solos. It also means building phrases that use similar, often cyclical, pitch structures. These are often referred to as motifs or themes. When you do this, your solo will sound symmetrical to a listener.

Like other art forms, the creation of symmetry and/or the breaking of symmetry yields interesting results. This is due to the fact that symmetry, and the repetition of symmetry, creates expectations that are emotionally reinforcing when met and emotionally painful when dashed.

A motif or theme is a short, relevant, melodic statement. The two components of a motif are melody and rhythm. For a motif to become meaningful, it must use a series of melodic intervals played in rhythm. When properly executed, this motif will stamp itself in the musical consciousness of the listener. Once established, the motif can—and often should—be repeated, either in exact duplication or with variation. When using variation, the rhythm and the pitches can be varied or transformed in some way. Ultimately, the goal is to set up expectations in the mind of the listener and then, for effect, meet them or not.

When improvising, this approach is the glue that holds a solo together. It certainly helps you to avoid playing strings of unconnected, disjointed musical statements. The best way to learn how to modify a motif is through example. In **FIGURES 11–4** and **11–7**, you'll see (and hear) how this is done. Notice how symmetry is established and developed over the course of the exercise. This is done through intervallic and rhythmical variation.

FIGURE 11–4.
Modal motif 1

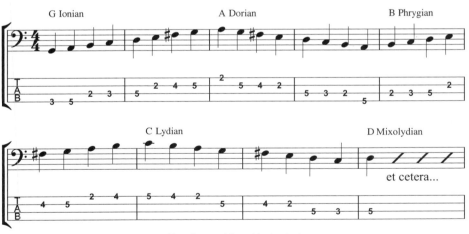

Experiment with positioning too!

FIGURE 11–5.
Modal motif 2

et cetera...

Experiment with positioning and fingering!

FIGURE 11–6. Modal and rhythmic motif 1

TRACK 29

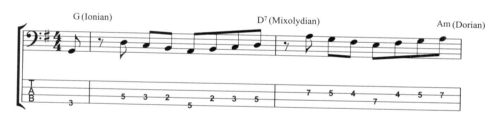

The rhythms make the modes come alive!

FIGURE 11–7.
Modal and
rhythmic
motif 2

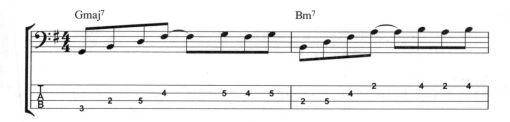

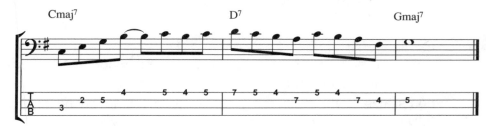

You decide what the modes are!

Soloing in Blues and Rock

Since blues and rock have many similarities, it's convenient and practical to take a look at them in conjunction. Rock is derived from the blues; therefore, you should get comfortable with soloing over the standard twelve-bar blues forms. Even if you're only interested in rock, the twelve-bar blues is a crucial form to know.

Soloing over a blues progression is one of the most natural ways to improvise. There is something about the blues that nearly everyone seems to have some affinity for. It's actually possible to solo over an entire blues progression with one scale. But in order to have complete success with a blues solo, you still have to make sure that you know the twelve-bar form cold. Make sure you review Chapter 8 so that you get a refresher course on this. Once you feel completely comfortable with the blues form, you might want to experiment with more than just one scale. In fact, it's common to quote several scales during a blues solo. However, if you're not sure what to play, use only one scale. This can often be the most effective and direct method of communication.

QUESTION?

What scales can I use in a blues solo?

Although there are many scales that can be employed, there are four basic scales that are most commonly used in blues music: minor and major pentatonics and minor and major blues scales. All of these scales are extremely similar, and their minor and major forms observe the rules of musical relativity (see Chapters 8 and 9).

Although you were introduced to major and minor pentatonics in Chapter 9, **FIGURES 11–8** and **11–9** review major and minor pentatonic, closed-position scales. In these figures, you have a chance to extend each scale as fully as possible in each position. That means that you will extend the scale beyond one full octave. In some cases you will extend the scale above the octave. In other cases you will extend the scale both above and below each tonic pitch. The notes that go beyond the true octaves of each scale are written in parentheses.

FIGURE 11–8.

Two closed-position major pentatonic scales fully extended

Notes that go beyond the true octaves of each scale are written in parentheses.

FIGURE 11–9.

Two closed-position minor pentatonic scales fully extended

A Minor Pentatonic

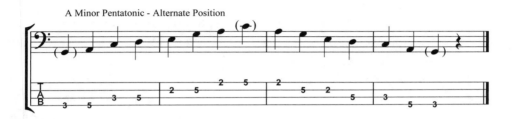

A Minor Pentatonic - Alternate Position

Blues Scales and Applications

Now you are ready to take a look at the blues scales. The only difference between these scales and pentatonic scales is one note: the almighty "blue" note.

FACT

For minor blues scales, the "blue" note is the same as the diminished fifth you learned in Chapter 10. When learning how to use blues scales, it may be easier to focus on the minor scales first. Once you've mastered these, simply shift down three half steps (or frets) and maintain the same position and pattern. When you do this, you will be playing the major blues scale of the same letter name.

After you've located the blue note, or flatted fifth, you are ready to try the minor blues scale. Again, this scale is exactly like the minor pentatonic from Chapter 9 except that the scale now includes the additional blue note. **FIGURE 11–10** shows you the fully extended version of this scale (with E-flats acting as blue notes). Again, notes that go beyond the true octaves of each scale are written in parentheses. You will also see parentheses in the same way on **FIGURES 11–11** through **11–14**.

FIGURE 11–10.
A-minor blues
scale fully
extended in
closed position

Next, replay the same shape or pattern on the neck and think of it as the relative major blues scale. How does this work? The two scales use the same set of notes. When you use the position illustrated in **FIGURE 11–10**, the second note in the minor scale (C) becomes the tonic of the relative major scale. It's interesting to see that these scales use the same shapes and pitches. The difference lies in the emphasis on a tonic. This is shown in **FIGURE 11–11**. Remember, the tonic is C. In the previous figure the tonic was A.

FIGURE 11–11.
C-major blues
scale fully
extended in
closed position

Although this scale begins on an A the tonic pitch is C!

After comparing the relative minor and major blues scales, you should compare major and minor blues scales of the same letter name. These are called parallel major and minor keys (as opposed to relative major/minor). To shift from the minor blues scale to the major one, all you need to do is to shift the same pattern down three frets. This is shown in **FIGURE 11–12**.

Of course, if you know other positions for each scale, you can play a major blues scale in the exact same location that you find the minor blues scale. However, make sure you use the proper intervallic model for each scale. Check out **FIGURES 11–13** and **11–14**. Here the positions and shapes of the scale overlap. Of course, there are dozens of other positions for you to explore, and you should experiment with them until you discover and internalize as many of them as possible.

FIGURE 11–12.
Comparing A-minor and A-major blues scales

In this figure, the A-major blues scale does not begin on the tonic pitch, but rather, the sixth scale degree (F#).

FIGURE 11–13.
Comparing A-minor and A-major blues scales in overlapping positions

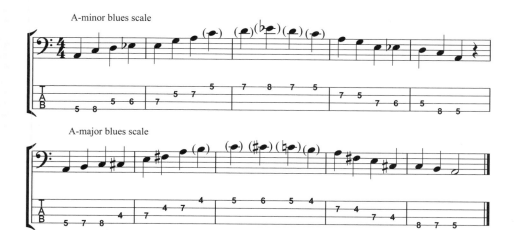

FIGURE 11–14.

More comparisons of A-minor and A-major blues scales in overlapping positions

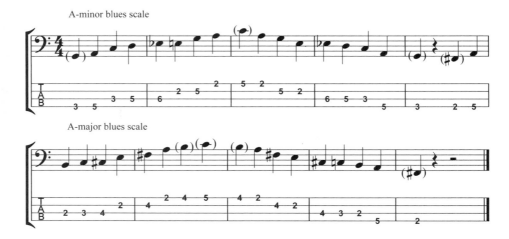

A-minor blues scale

A-major blues scale

Integrating Scales

Even though the blues is relatively simple to solo over, you may still have stumbling blocks. The key is integrating all of these scales in a convincing way. In some cases, one scale is more appropriate than another. In other cases, it is more effective to mix the scales in ways that form hybrid combinations. By experimenting with these combinations, and listening carefully to the outcomes, you can discover where each scale works best.

ALERT!

The minor pentatonic and blues scales are almost exactly the same. Moreover, they both work well on just about any blues or blues rock form. On the other hand, the major pentatonic and major blues scales should be used more sparingly unless they are switched on every chord so that the scale and the chord names match.

When you creatively combine all these scales, either in chunks or as hybrids, and then perform them as musical phrases, motifs, or riffs, you start to get something that sounds like a basic blues solo. If you combine that with an imaginative use of rhythm, which is a common characteristic of the blues, you'll have even more fun. **FIGURE 11–15** is a solo that combines all these many elements.

FIGURE 11–15. Basic twelve-bar blues solo

Note: Even though Figure 11-15 is an A major blues, the key signature used here is C major since it's easier to read. Major blues scales use both major and minor thirds and minor (dominant) seventh intervals. If this etude were written in A major, you would be reading an overabundance of natural symbols.

Tying It All Together

In order to apply what you've learned to rock, all you need to do is expand your imagination and hone in on the style of rock that you are trying to express. One thing that may differentiate a rock solo from a blues solo is the level of aggression. Sometimes an aggressive rock performance is achieved by playing fast. Generally speaking, the blues tends to be less concerned with flashy, fast licks.

Sometimes the aggressive sound of a rock solo is achieved by using effects and volume. For example, bassists might use distortion or effects pedals, which alter the timbre (tone color) of the instrument. In short, if you're playing blues licks but you've got the volume cranked up to ten and the distortion full bore, your solo may sound rock oriented. However, if you're playing with a more intimate, clean sound your solo may sound bluesier.

Lastly, rock tunes don't always use twelve-bar blues forms. In fact, most contemporary rock songs do not. Rock tunes can venture anywhere and draw from virtually any style of music. Because of this, you have to be ready to incorporate all different kinds of sounds and scales into your rock playing. In addition to regular pentatonic and blues scales, jazzy modes (Dorian, Mixolydian, Lydian, and so on) may help you to expand your rock horizons.

At this point, it's best to illustrate these concepts with as many examples as possible. **FIGURE 11–16** shows aggression through speed, repetition, and the attack of the performance.

FIGURE 11–16.
Rock lick using aggression, speed, and repetition

Be sure to play forcefully so that this lick sounds like rock!

FIGURE 11–17 uses a chord progression that deviates far from the blues. Here, modes and pentatonic/blues scales work well.

FIGURE 11–18 uses repetition and rhythmic complexity to create tension and release.

Soloing in Jazz and Latin

Although jazz and Latin are not the same, in many instances the soloing styles for both are similar. Since Latin has been influenced to a large extent by jazz, especially in Brazilian and Afro-Cuban styles, the general rules of

FIGURE 11–17. Rock licks over a chord progression

TRACK 31

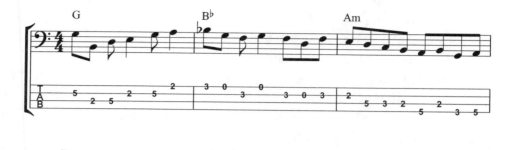

FIGURE 11–18. Rock licks with tension and release

TRACK 32

jazz soloing apply to Latin soloing. The only caveat here is that jazz often has a swing feel, whereas Latin almost always uses straight eighths (see Chapter 8). For all the exercises in this section, it's advisable to play them with a swing and a straight-eighth feel.

Pulling off a compelling improvised solo in jazz is one of the hardest feats in all of musical performance. The following five figures start you off on the right foot.

You should also practice assimilating the chords and scales that you already know. Try to attach a scale to each type of chord. The simplest way to address this is to play the first mode, Ionian, on the first, or I, chord. Then play the second mode, Dorian, on the second, or ii, chord, and so on. For the fifth, or V, chord, play a Mixolydian mode. **FIGURE 11–19** illustrates this concept using a ii–V–I chord progression. Bear in mind that you'll almost always use only a snippet of the mode because there won't be enough time to play the whole scale.

FIGURE 11–19. Using modes on a ii–V–I chord progression

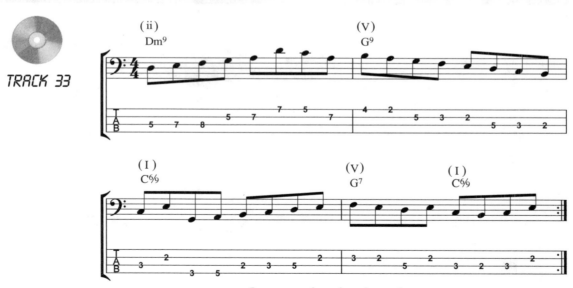

TRACK 33

Roman numerals are shown in parentheses.

Let's reduce this down to an even simpler formula. Because the modes all use the same notes just in a different order, all you really need to use is one scale: the major scale of the I chord. So when you see a major ii–V–I, you may simply use variations of the major scale of the I chord over the entire progression. It all comes down to how you conceive of the notes in the scales. Remember, scales can always be reconfigured or played from different start points.

Next, add a few more ingredients. Start by including broken chords or arpeggios. Then add a new chord extension called the ninth. The ninth is really the same note as the second except it is shifted one octave higher. In **FIGURE 11–20**, you will see expanded arpeggios using ninths.

FIGURE 11–20.
Different chords with ninths

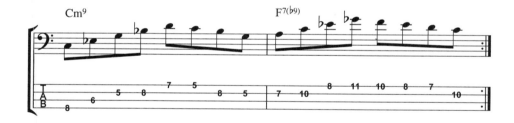

Now add in chromatics. Start by placing a nondiatonic, chromatic half step—one that is not part of the original mode/scale—on the weak beat. This is called an *outside* chromatic. For example, put the outside chromatic on the "and" when playing eighth notes. Also, be sure to end the melodic phrase on a strong or colorful note. This is exhibited in **FIGURES 11–21** and **11–22**.

There is still much to learn in the jazz and Latin realm, and much more information will be presented to you over the next several chapters. There are certain chords that you don't know how to deal with quite yet. However, **FIGURE 11–23** (on the following page) puts it all together so far.

FIGURE 11–21.
Chromatic
solo line 1

End this passage on beat one of the first measure!

FIGURE 11–22.
Chromatic
solo line 2

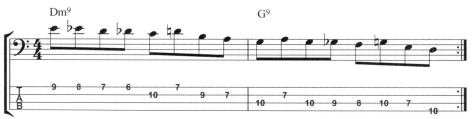

Try ending this passage on a C.

FIGURE 11–23. Jazz solo over standard chord changes

TRACK 34

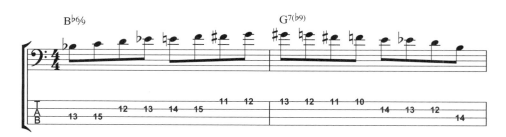

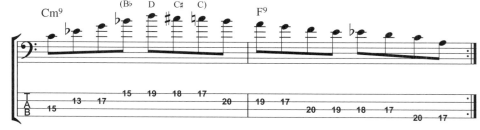

This figure uses the highest notes on the bass. If you wish, you may play the pattern an octave lower.

Chapter 12
Fun Licks and Lines

Musical motifs and clichés make up the basic vocabulary of all genres of music. These common riffs and melodic patterns define what is appropriate and what is not in any given style. In every genre, there are hundreds of licks and lines that you can use. All totaled, these licks comprise each style's musical lexicon. The ones you select and emphasize—as opposed to the ones you omit—contribute to your individual voice. Additionally, your signature sound results from the unique variations or twists that you bring to the musical conversation.

Down-Home Blues Lines

When in Paris, you'd be well advised to know how to speak French. Likewise, when playing the blues, you'd better know how to speak its musical language. The blues is a place where you'll find bold individuality melded with the most strident use of musical cliché. In other words, there is, simultaneously, a mix of great personal freedom and strict adherence to tradition and conformity.

For the bassist, blues is an idiom where the shuffling, walking bass line is king. Although soloing does occur, blues bassists are not generally required to perform outlandish feats of technical prowess. More likely, a bassist might use his solo to simply play a slightly more interesting version of his walking bass line (with a few cool licks thrown in). At the end of the day, the highly regarded blues bassist is the one who holds down the fort. His most important job is to keep great time through rock solid bass lines.

As you might imagine, there are some important cliché bass lines in the blues. You learned some of these already in Chapters 7, 8, and 9, where blues forms the basis for those genres discussed. However, this is just the tip of the iceberg.

FIGURE 12–1 shows a walking pattern moving up and down on a dominant seventh chord. Take note of the extensive use of chromatics. This bass line is often used on the I7 chord in a blues progression. This pattern can also be altered so that it transitions into a IV7 chord on beat one of measure five. In order to do this, swap out the last two notes for pitches that, instead, move in the direction of the IV7 chord. For example, you might alter beat four of measure four to E- or C-sharp, then play D on beat one of the fifth bar. In this case, D is the root of the IV7 chord.

FIGURE 12–1.
Common walking bass line for a I7 chord

There are many small variations on the standard twelve-bar blues. If you include jazz, there are some extensive variations. But leaving jazz aside, one of the most common modifications of the twelve-bar blues form in the Chicago style involves substituting different chords in measures nine and ten. Instead of measures nine and ten using the V7 chord and the IV7 chord, respectively, you can use a ii7 (minor) in measure nine and a V7 chord in measure ten. There are numerous ways to walk between these, but another common blues pattern using chromatics is seen in **FIGURE 12–2**, which has both an ascending and descending walking bass line. As always, experiment with alterations to these basic templates. This will help you to find your own voice as a bassist.

FIGURE 12–2.
Walking between a ii7 and V7 in measures nine and ten of a twelve-bar blues line

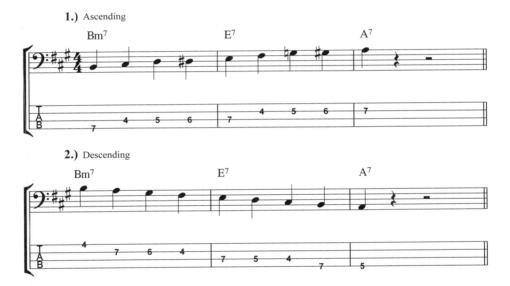

There are many other simple blues bass lines that really work. One example is illustrated in **FIGURE 12–3**. Here you'll see the use of a one-five-seven bass line where the intervals include the tonic, the fifth, and the dominant seventh. Two versions of this bass line have been notated for you. The first pattern ends on the tonic (measure one). The second ends on the fifth (measure two).

FIGURE 12–3.

Using a one-five-seven bass line two ways

Lastly, you need to know how to end the blues. **FIGURE 12–4** illustrates two common blues endings: one ascending and one descending. As with all these blues figures, please experiment with rhythmic variation. For example, try them with straight eighths, swing eighths, a quarter-note walking feel, and as hard shuffles.

FIGURE 12–4.

Two blues endings

Hardcore Rock Licks

Rock is a genre that is sometimes known for hotshot solos and other fast licks. Bass guitar pyrotechnics go back to the days of psychedelic rock where Jack Bruce (Cream) and John Paul Jones (Led Zeppelin) developed licks and bass lines that changed the role of bass in rock. Through the years, people like Chris Squire (Yes), Geddy Lee (Rush), and Billy Sheehan (Talas, Mr. Big, Niacin) have also upped the ante on just what it means to be a great rock bassist.

The early progenitors of this more ambitious style of bass playing often used a combination of driving attack and fast, funky arpeggios. **FIGURE 12–5** exemplifies this through a simulation of John Paul Jones's style. This example only captures the basics of Jones's approach.

FIGURE 12–5.
Late-sixties-style hard rock bass line

Later, as progressive rock bloomed, bassists' musical vocabulary and adventurism expanded to all ends of the musical spectrum. Influences as diverse as classical, jazz, and world music were often incorporated into one long, epic composition. One scale that epitomizes the neoclassicism of progressive rock is the harmonic minor scale. Heavy metal bands with a progressive slant (Deep Purple and Iron Maiden) also use this scale.

QUESTION?

How many minor scales are there?

There are three traditional minor scales. In Chapter 4, you learned about the natural minor scale. The other traditional minor scales are the harmonic minor and the melodic minor. There are also many more minor scales that are modal and less common. These are used mainly in ethnic styles of music and in contemporary jazz.

The harmonic minor scale is the same as the natural minor scale except that its seventh scale degree is raised one half step; for bassists, that means one fret higher on the neck. Play and listen carefully to the A harmonic minor scale shown in **FIGURE 12–6**.

FIGURE 12–6.
The A harmonic minor scale

The chords written above the scale show its relationship to harmony.

Using the Harmonic Minor Scale

The harmonic minor scale can accommodate minor-key chord progressions that use a major, dominant chord (V chord). However, in most progressive rock and metal, the usage of the harmonic minor is more a matter of taste. Because the harmonic minor has a uniquely large interval (an augmented second) between the sixth and seventh tones, it has an exotic flavor reminiscent of Middle Eastern music.

It's fun to improvise or solo using this scale. It can also be used for constructing bass lines. In **FIGURE 12–7**, you'll play some licks using this exotic, and even pompous sounding, scale. The licks in **FIGURE 12–7** are designed to sound like improvisations.

FIGURE 12–7.
Exotic licks using the harmonic minor

Here, the G sharp makes these licks sound exotic!

Tapping and Pull-Offs

Another technique or style that gives you that rock edge is to play fast, repetitive, minor-scale arpeggios or pentatonic licks using either hammer-ons (see Chapter 9) or two-handed tapping techniques. Popularized by guitarist Eddie Van Halen, two-handed tapping came into vogue in the early 1980s and 1990s and was adopted by a fair number of bassists as well as guitarists. The tapping technique requires you to bring your picking hand over the neck. If you're playing right-handed bass, you play hammer-on notes using the fingers in your right hand. This is done in conjunction with the left hand, which usually plays two additional notes. Another way to get this type of sound without tapping is to use the left hand in a pull-off fashion in conjunction with open strings. **FIGURE 12–8** illustrates this type of lick. Of course, simply playing scales or pentatonics with high speed and technical proficiency will always dazzle a rock audience, as long as good taste and judiciousness are used.

FIGURE 12–8. Pull-off licks that impress

TRACK 35

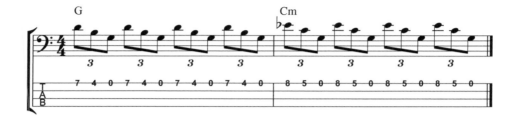

Dazzling Funk and R & B Licks

Scales, walking bass patterns, and syncopations form the cornerstone of most R & B styles. But it's how you use them that matters the most! Start by reviewing the major and minor pentatonic and blues scales found in Chapters 9 and 11. You have to really understand and be comfortable with these scales before you can progress further. One of the most important steps is to be able to navigate these scales separately, to understand the difference between them, and to know where and when each scale should be used.

ALERT!

It's important to clarify the use of the pentatonic and blues scales. If you have a major chord, you can use both the major and minor pentatonic scales. The same is true of blues scales. However, if you have a minor chord, and you wish to only use pentatonics or blues scales, you must only use the minor version of each scale.

Combining the major and minor pentatonic/blues scales produces one of the most compelling bass lines that you can use in R & B and funk. This works only on major chords, because with minor chords you can only use a minor scale(s). Keep in mind that the emphasis here is on major chords with dominant sevenths. This concept does not apply to major chords with major sevenths. That's a whole other ball game!

FIGURE 12–9 shows you how to combine major and minor pentatonic and blues scales. In this example, you'll see a lick that really mixes it up. There is something extra funky about a bass line that combines rhythmic syncopation and dexterous melodicism.

FIGURE 12–9.
Combining
scales in funk

Ostinatos, Double Stops, and Slaps

Another musical device that is supremely funky, especially as epitomized by the compositions of James Brown, is the use of ostinatos (see Chapter 8). The note-for-note repetition of a bass line without almost any variation is one of the hallmarks of Brown's brand of soulful R & B. **FIGURE 12–10** attempts to recreate an ostinato bass line that Bootsy Collins, one of James Brown's bassists, might have played.

FIGURE 12–10.
Funky ostinato
bass groove

Another device to keep in your musical toolbox is something called a *double stop*. A double stop is when you play two notes at once. In R & B and funk, a double stop can provide a really funky accent to whatever you are normally playing. The most important interval used as a double stop in funk and R & B is the diminished fifth or flatted five (see Chapter 10). The other name for this interval is a tritone.

Tritones have many uses (especially in jazz); however, in funk and R & B, the tritone is representative of two essential notes from the dominant seventh chord. If you have a major chord with a dominant seventh—for example A7—pick out the third and the dominant seven and play them as a double-stop. On an A7 chord, you would play a C-sharp and a G in any configuration.

FACT

The tritone's symmetry holds true in any inversion. In other words, if you find either the third or the seventh and play the same shape on the fretboard of the bass guitar, you'll derive the proper intervals every time. Moreover, it doesn't matter if the third is on top (higher) or if the seventh is on top. It still works out!

The best way to use a double stop is to play it in the higher range of the bass. This keeps it from sounding too muddy. Also, it's common to slide into the double stop when you play it. **FIGURE 12–11** illustrates just how the double stop can fit into your bass lines or licks. Notice the use of tritones with the third on top and one with the seventh on the top. Most importantly, notice how they sound essentially the same. They are also exactly the same shape.

FIGURE 12–11. Funky tritone double stops

TRACK 36

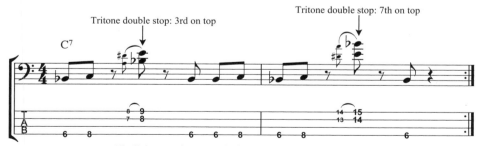

The little notes that appear before the double stops are grace notes.
They tell you to slide into the double stops!

In Chapter 9 you learned about slap technique. Obviously, this is a funky and flashy way to add a lick or to supercharge a bass line. Even if you are playing with your fingers, you can throw in a snap or pop here and there or switch to the slap technique for a bar or two. **FIGURE 12–12** uses all of these techniques. Be sure to use these techniques on your own lines and licks too. Improvisation is an essential component for bass competency.

FIGURE 12–12. Adding some snap to your funk

TRACK 37

Be sure to listen to this example on the CD to hear the various finger techniques used!

Snaky Jazz and Latin Licks

For all intents and purposes, the kinds of licks that you might use in a Latin jam are equal to those you might use in a jazz session. In fact, jazz electric bassists often play Latin grooves and fast sambas. In fusion jazz, it is common to almost never swing but instead to play grooves borrowed from Latin, funk, and rock. Jaco Pastorius, whom you learned about in Chapter 8, was one of the great pioneers of fusion. He was also extremely deft on a Latin tune.

To play jazz and Latin licks and lines it takes practice and a lot of study. Unlike rock, blues, and even R & B/funk, jazz and Latin require true erudition. Unless you're a natural born genius, you can't just use your ears to learn how to play in these idioms. Furthermore, to be able to improvise a hot jazz or Latin lick you will need to really steep yourself in the cultures of these styles. Luckily, in this chapter, and throughout the rest of the book, you'll learn some tricks of the trade that can help you demystify and unlock the secrets to creating jazz and Latin lines and licks.

The first thing that will help you put some snaky jazz and Latin licks and lines together is another scale. This scale is extremely versatile and multipurpose. Without a doubt, it can immediately bring your jazz skills up about ten notches. What is this scale? It is the almighty melodic minor.

The Melodic Minor Scale

Comprising the final piece of the minor scale tripartite, the melodic minor is distinguished from the natural minor by its raised sixth and seventh scale degrees (see **FIGURE 12–13**). Traditionally, the scale is performed with these raised sixth and seventh tones only when ascending. When descending, it is traditional to revert to the natural minor, as in **FIGURE 12–13**. However, in jazz you can also play the scale using the same notes when descending. In other words, retain the raised sixth and seventh tones throughout. In the remaining figures, you'll notice that the raised tones are always retained. As in **FIGURE 12–6**, the melodic minor scale shown below is not fully extended throughout the position. It is hoped that you are now capable of extrapolating the extended position from the one-octave version shown here.

FIGURE 12–13.
The A melodic
minor scale

The chords written above the scale show its relationship to harmony.

This scale's most obvious use is on the i chord in a minor key. In subsequent chapters you will be taught more about working in minor keys. For now, simply recognize that there are major and minor keys. Major keys are based on major scales, which have their own diatonic triads and chord progressions (for example, ii–V–I chord changes). Minor keys are the same. However, they are based on a minor scale with chord functions extending up i through vii, or i through VII depending on the type of minor key used. Remember, lowercase Roman numerals indicate minor. Uppercase Roman numerals indicate major.

Just as in major keys, minor keys also have similar chord progressions, such as ii–V–i progression. The melodic minor scale seen in Figure 12-13 is used for a i chord in a minor key. Therefore, it could be used on an Am, or using jazz extensions, on an Am6/9 or Amin(maj7). In this musical context, it's pretty easy to decide what melodic minor scale to use. For example, if you are in the key of A minor, you will play licks using an A melodic minor on the i chord. In other words, an Am6/9 chord would use an A melodic minor.

However, this is just the beginning. Basically, this scale has three other uses. It can also be used on a ii chord in a minor key, a V chord in a minor key, and a V chord in a major key. This is fascinating because the melodic minor can be used on all the chords in a minor ii–V–i progression and on one of the chords in a major ii–V–I progression. Unfortunately, it's hard to know what melodic minor scales to use in these contexts. In fact, the melodic minors that are used may be quite different from what you might expect. **FIGURE 12–14** shows a minor ii–V–i progression in A minor together with the appropriate melodic minor scales used to create jazz lines. In Chapter 17, you'll crack the code to figure out what melodic minor scales are used on similar progressions.

FIGURE 12–14. Minor ii–V–i progression with corresponding melodic minor scales

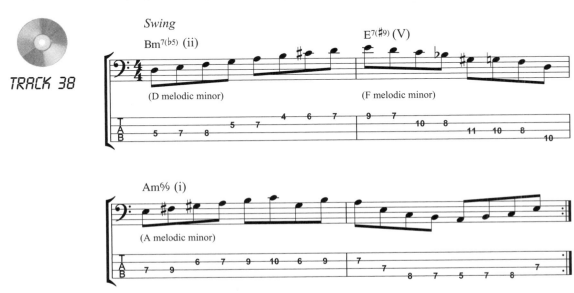

TRACK 38

As was stated previously, melodic minor scales can also be used on V chords in a major key in jazz, fusion, or Latin. These are usually seen as V7, V9, or V13. On these chords, you would not use the melodic minor with the same letter name. In other words, if you have a G7, you would not use a G melodic minor scale. Instead, you would use the scale found a perfect fifth (7 half steps or frets) above the name of the chord. In the case of a G7, you would use a D melodic minor.

FIGURES 12–15 and **12–16** expresses this idea through notation. As you move forward in this book, you'll learn more about the details and theory behind jazz and Latin playing; however, the melodic minor may be the best kept secret of them all.

FIGURE 12–15. Using the melodic minor on a V chord in a major key

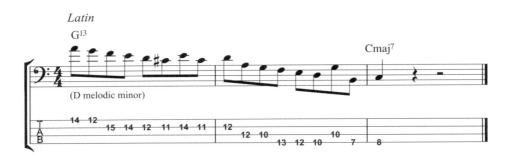

FIGURE 12–16. Using the melodic minor on any dominant seventh chord

TRACK 39

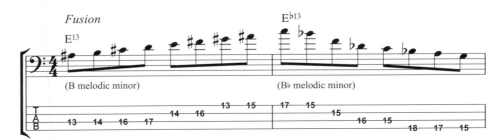

Chapter 13
Study Pieces

Most of the figures in this book are brief. Many include a phrase or two. Others feature an ostinato pattern or a lick. However, this chapter comprises in-depth study pieces. In other words, the four etudes here expand upon many of the techniques and concepts you've learned in previous chapters. Given the longer format of each piece, you will want to spend extra time practicing these etudes. You should also learn these pieces in the order in which they appear since they get progressively harder.

The Legacy of Willie Dixon

Willie Dixon (1915–1992) was one of the most important figures in the blues, and his impact on the bass cannot be underestimated. In addition to his upright bass playing, Dixon's songwriting and producing skills further enhance his presence as one of the most pivotal characters in the blues.

Dixon was born in Vicksburg, Mississippi, a small city located in the Mississippi Delta. It was in the Mississippi Delta that the blues was born around 1900. In the early 1900s, no one knew that the blues would become one of the world's most influential styles of music, playing a significant role in the development of jazz, rock, and popular styles. However, the great migration north to Chicago gave the blues a lasting voice in popular music. Along with Muddy Waters, Howlin' Wolf, and others, Dixon was one of the Delta bluesmen to move to Chicago in the 1930s. Once there, he helped to create the Chicago style of blues.

FACT

The Great Migration occurred after both world wars in the United States. This movement is critical to the development of all forms of African American music. It was in the metropolitan areas of northern cities such as Chicago, Detroit, and New York that the blues crossed racial barriers and captured the American consciousness. Willie Dixon was an integral part of this musical revolution.

As a songwriter, Dixon penned some of the most memorable blues numbers in history, including "Hoochie Coochie Man," "I Just Want to Make Love to You," and many others. Rock legends Led Zeppelin borrowed from Dixon's song "You Need Love" to create their hit "Whole Lotta Love." A 1985 lawsuit gave Dixon credit as co-composer.

Looking at Dixon's career in retrospective, it's clear that Dixon had a great impact on rock and pop music. First of all, he played bass on many early Chuck Berry records. Secondly, dozens of rock and pop artists have covered Dixon's tunes. Some notables include the Doors, Eric Clapton, the Grateful Dead, the Rolling Stones, Cream, the Monkees, Aerosmith, Megadeth, the Jesus and Mary Chain, and P. J. Harvey.

Blues for Willie Dixon

As a bassist, Dixon created many of the blues clichés we now consider standard fare. For example, he helped to define simple walking bass lines in jump-blues. One of the techniques he used on up-tempo songs was a right hand slapping approach. This gave the bass a percussive feel and a much louder tone. As you learn about Dixon's playing in the following etude, remember that he was an upright bassist. The upright bass, or bass violin, is considerably different from the electric bass guitar. Bass guitarists have long since appropriated Dixon's elegant yet aggressive bass style, so his playing should not be overlooked or deemphasized in your studies.

FIGURE 13–1, "Blues for Willie Dixon," mimics the slow, down-home blues ballad style that was played in Chicago in the 1940s and 1950s. Here you will see swing eighth notes. As you know from previous chapters, this means that you should give the music a flowing triplet feel. Like the playing of Dixon, this piece uses both long and short notes. This creates a rhythmical contrast that gives the bass line needed forward momentum. For example, in the first full measure you will see a half note followed by a staccato quarter note. (Staccato is indicated by the small dot under the note head.) Be sure to clip the quarter note short when you see the staccato symbol. This technique will make your blues bass lines more expressive and dramatic.

In this etude, you will also see grace notes. These are the miniature notes that precede certain quarter and eighth notes. Grace notes are used constantly in the blues and other styles of music. Grace notes help to create a sliding or glissando affect. Sliding into notes is essential. If you don't use grace notes, your playing will sound stiff.

Also notice the use of major and minor pentatonics throughout the etude together with judicious chromatic movement. As you learned in Chapter 9, pentatonics, or five-note scales, form the basis for bass riffs and lines in many styles, especially in blues, jazz, and rock. Finally, the last two measures of the piece employ a clichéd blues ending. You should memorize this ending and use it when you create your own blues bass lines. Common blues endings, like this one, root your playing in the culture and history of the music. Remember, the blues is a mixture of fierce individualism and tried and true formulas.

FIGURE 13–1. "Blues for Willie Dixon"

TRACK 40

Blues for Willie Dixon

Swing

♩=70

By Nelson Starr

FIGURE 13–1. "Blues for Willie Dixon"

TRACK 40

Forever Paul

As you learned in Chapter 7, Paul McCartney is one of the most important bass players in history. Early on, McCartney played bass lines that included mostly roots and fifths. Yet despite the stock nature of his playing, McCartney's rhythmical precision and driving feel made songs such as "Please, Please Me" and "I Want to Hold Your Hand" unique and indelible.

Around 1967, with the release of *Sgt. Pepper's Lonely Hearts Club Band*, McCartney's bass playing became much more melodic. He did this by incorporating scalar runs and arpeggios into his bass lines. This added greater texture and harmonic nuance to the Beatles' music. McCartney's evolution as a bass player (and songwriter) owes much to Brian Wilson. Wilson was the songwriting mastermind behind the American singing group the Beach Boys. More than anything, Wilson's masterpiece *Pet Sounds* contributed to McCartney's melodic development on the bass. Much of this was also due to the incredible session work of bassist Carol Kaye.

FACT

Contemporary pressings of *Pet Sounds* (1966, Capital Records) by the Beach Boys include liner notes from Paul McCartney. In his commentary, McCartney states that *Pet Sounds* blew him out of the water. He also refers to the album as "the classic of the century." Further, McCartney states that the melodic bass lines on the album made him "sit up and take notice."

In **FIGURE 13–2**, you will see the melodic patterns McCartney uses to bring a bass line (and song!) to life. This etude is essentially an improvisation

FIGURE 13–2. "Forever Paul"

Forever Paul

By Nelson Starr

TRACK 41

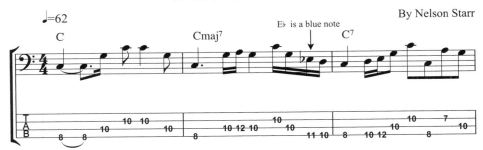

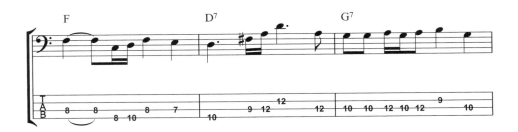

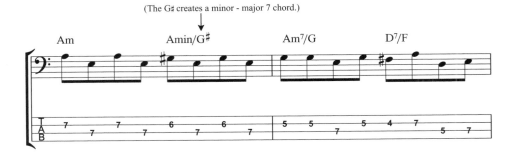

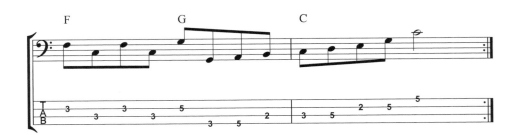

on the chord changes to "Something," a rock ballad from the album *Abbey Road*. The piece also employs some riffs similar to those used by McCartney on "Dear Prudence" from *The White Album*. These riffs appear in measures seven and eight. In measures seven and eight, you will also see chords that use slashes. These are called slash chords. With slash chords, the letter name that appears *after* the slash is an alternate bass note. When you see these, play the alternate bass note instead of the root of the chord.

Lastly, neobaroque *Sgt. Pepper*-influenced bass licks round out this etude in measures seven, eight, and nine. McCartney's neobaroque bass lines are created through the use of dropdown bass. Dropdown bass juxtaposes a descending bass line against a fixed chord. When doing this, bass lines move in whole steps, half steps, or a combination thereof. Dropdown bass lines create alternate bass notes on chords (slash chords) as they descend. This adds beautiful melodicism in the lower register of a piece. Baroque composers J. S. Bach and Antonio Vivaldi were among the first to use this contrapuntal device in the eighteenth century. In **FIGURE 13–2**, you will see a straight chromatic descent from A to G♯ to G to F♯ in measures seven and eight. This kind of dropdown bass is common in pop music.

When playing **FIGURE 13–2**, pick higher up on the neck. This will give you a distinct McCartney sound since you will produce a rounder tone. Also, you should roll off the tone knob to simulate the bass sound that McCartney used on later Beatles recordings. McCartney got this sound by using a Rickenbacker bass. This bass's distinctive tone is due in large part to the treble and bass tone controls.

Jazz Caliente

Bossa nova and salsa have long borrowed from jazz harmony. Afro-Cuban orchestras led by Dizzy Gillespie and others brought Latin jazz to the fore in the late 1940s and 1950s when traditional swing bands were on the decline. In some ways, the trend of combining Latin and jazz peaked with the Broadway musical *West Side Story* (1957). On this masterwork, composer Leonard Bernstein combined Afro-Cuban rhythms with jazzy harmony in a unique, accessible setting. Today Latin jazz continues to thrive though its cousin, Latin pop, overshadows it. Despite this, jazz artists such as Chick

Corea, Michelle Camilo, Paquito D'Rivera, Arturo Sandoval, Eliane Elias, Pat Metheny, and others regularly infuse their music with robust Latin flavors.

The next etude, "Jazz Caliente," combines an Afro-Cuban feel with a minor blues form. Merging blues forms with Latin is not uncommon in Latin jazz. **FIGURE 13–3** shows you the chord changes to a minor blues form. There are many variations on the minor blues formula; the most basic blues progression includes only i, iv, and V chords. But as you know, jazz is based on harmonic sophistication. It naturally craves chordal variation and dissonance. Therefore, the minor blues outlined in **FIGURE 13–3** shows you some chord possibilities with harmonic extensions, such as flat fives, dominant sevenths, sharp nines, and flat nines. Notice how measures ten and twelve give you the choice of a flat nine or a sharp nine. These extensions are virtually interchangeable. Also, remember the cardinal rule in the blues. With rare exception, the form is always twelve bars long.

FIGURE 13–3.
Minor blues form

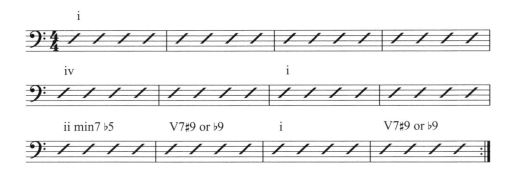

The basic pattern of "Jazz Caliente" (see **FIGURE 13–4**) revolves around the one-five-nine-ten intervallic set. If you look at the first four bars, you will see this arpeggio used on the Amin9 chords. Here the chords are broken up so that you play the root, the fifth, the major ninth, and the major tenth (sometimes just called a third). This could be turned into an ostinato all by itself and applied to one-chord Dorian jams (à la Carlos Santana). This pattern could also serve as the basis for other Latin grooves, such as bossa novas and sambas.

Rhythmically, you'll notice the use of dotted quarter note–eighth patterns. This rhythm is ubiquitous in both Brazilian and Afro-Cuban music, though it is by no means the only ostinato used by these styles.

Other harmonic components to this etude include a quick natural minor jaunt leading into the first iv chord. This is found on beats three and four of measure four. In several spots you will also see the use of leading tones. Leading tones can be used to transition from one chord to another. You may lead into a new root by playing a note one half step below the new chord or one half step above it. For example, bars six, nine, eighteen, and twenty-one scoop into the root of the next measure from below. This is achieved by using leading tones on the "ands" of beat four. Leading tones from above are evident in measures six and eighteen (both dropping into E7-type chords). However, in this case they both fall on the "and" of beat two.

Another device used in bar fourteen is a half-step chord shift. If you look at this measure, you'll see that the Amin9 chord suddenly shifts into a B-flat min9 chord. This technique is common in both jazz and Latin. Half-step chord shifts create tension and excitement, and in an ensemble context they add a sudden burst of bitonality. The bitonality occurs as two chords—situated one half step apart—overlap briefly. Why does this happen? When you shift upward, the rest of the band may still be playing the original chord. You might think that would sound awful, but the reverse is actually true since the half-step chord shift is momentary. Playing half-step chord shifts actually creates interesting leading tones as well as emotional anticipation. In this case, the listener waits for the raised chord to drop back into its proper place. For example, in measure fourteen, the high B-flat on beat four acts, for all intents and purposes, as a more dramatic and suspenseful kind of leading tone.

Last but not least, take note of the knotty arpeggio in measure twenty-four. This lick uses both intervallic jumps and chromatics. Try creating your own closing riffs that mimic the Latin music you hear. Don't know what to listen to? See Appendix A for a few suggestions.

FIGURE 13–4. "Jazz Caliente"

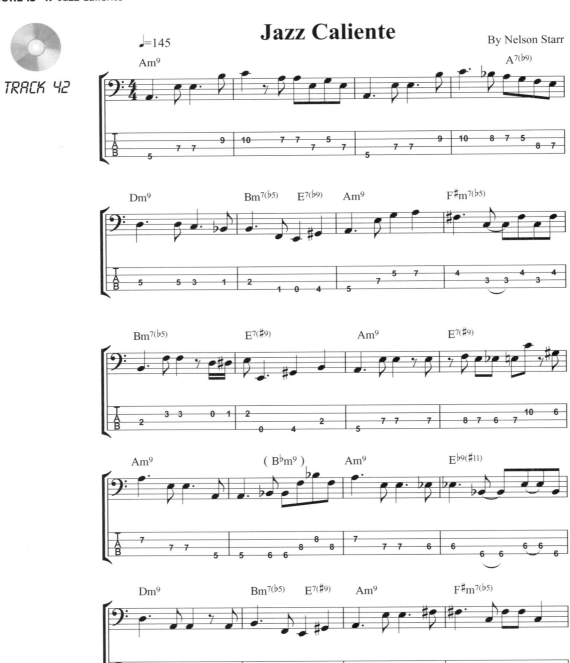

FIGURE 13–4. "Jazz Caliente"

TRACK 42

Jaco Lives

As discussed in Chapter 8, Jaco Pastorius (1951–1987) is a pivotal figure in jazz bass. Virtually every music student who plays electric bass tries to copy Jaco's style at some point. Unfortunately, the great Jaco Pastorius led a very troubled life, and due to a combination of mental illness and substance abuse he died at the young age of thirty-five.

The last etude found in this chapter was written in homage to the master bassist. Without a doubt, it is the hardest etude in this chapter and one of the most advanced pieces found in this book. Because of this, it is highly recommended that you learn this piece in sections or phrases, and be sure to listen to the CD to hear how it should sound.

There are a number of technical challenges in "Jaco Lives." First, the piece is played with a rubato feel in the beginning. *Rubato* means to play music without a pulse or tempo. In other words, you have the freedom to move through each phrase at your own discretion. Rubato allows for a lot of expression and nuance when playing. In contrast, beginning on measure eight you should move into a steady pulse. The notation simply states "In tempo" to give you some freedom regarding speed; however, you don't want to play these passages too slowly. Again, listen to the CD to get a sense for what tempos are appropriate.

Harmonically, this etude uses one-five-nine and one-five-ten arpeggios. This means that you will play root-fifth-ninth intervals and root-fifth-tenth intervals. For example, a root-fifth-ninth arpeggio starts the whole piece off in measure one. You will also see the use of harmonics. If you are new to harmonics, go back to Chapter 8 and learn this technique before trying to play **FIGURE 13–5**. To reproduce Jaco's signature style, you must use harmonics since they are integral to his sound. Bear in mind that interspersing harmonics with regular pitches is a special challenge. In fact, this requires a lot of patience, practice, and perseverance. (At first, some of your harmonics might not ring out as beautifully as you want them to.) However, developing the ability to use pitch contrast—highs and lows—on the bass will allow you many more options as a soloist no matter what style of music you play.

Other devices in "Jaco Lives" include bebop lines and funk clichés. For example, beat four of measure nine uses a melodic twist with a flat nine. This kind of turn is common in bop. On measure eight, you'll also see descending pentatonic patterns. Jaco loved using pentatonics since they create a truly funky sound. Rhythmically, you will see sixteenth notes and sixteenth rests used on a single pedal (E) on measures twelve through fifteen. This passage emulates Jaco's fondness for syncopation and funk! The sixteenth-note triplets used on the penultimate bar are also a Jaco trademark. For example, listen to Jaco's performance on the closing bars of Joni Mitchell's "Dry Cleaner from Des Moines" off of her 1979 release *Mingus*. On this tune, you will hear the meticulousness of Jaco's triplets.

FIGURE 13–5. "Jaco Lives"

Jaco Lives

By Nelson Starr

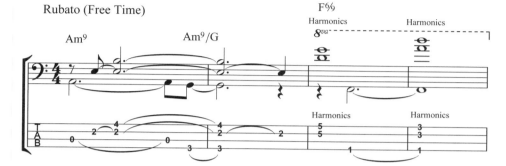

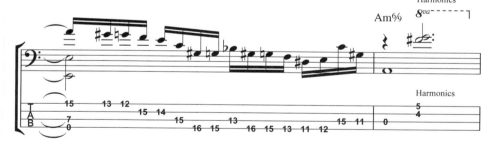

FIGURE 13–5. "Jaco Lives"

TRACK 43

8va ----⌐ tells you to play the notes one octave *higher* than written and it is used for ease in reading the notation. In this etude, this marking applies only to harmonics.

The Diminished Scale

The Jaco Pastorius etude in **FIGURE 13–5** opens up one additional can of worms: the diminished scale. Specifically, this etude uses a diminished scale on the altered V chord in measures five and six. A diminished scale is an exotic and snaky mode. These scales are made up of alternating whole and half steps. Figure 13-6 shows three versions of this scale.

FIGURE 13–6.
Three diminished scales

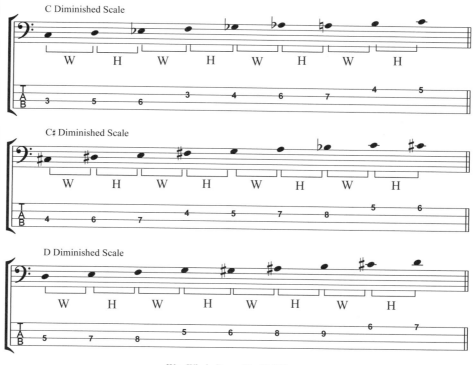

W = Whole Step   H = Half Step

Notice how all three of the diminished scales in **FIGURE 13–6** follow the whole-half intervallic model. For this reason, these scales are often called whole-half scales. You will usually hear jazz musicians using this term.

Music theorists usually call the diminished scale an octatonic scale because of the eight distinct pitches that characterize it. The diatonic modes, such as Ionian and Dorian, only use seven pitches. It is also possible to begin each diminished scale with a half-step interval. This type of octatonic scale is often called a half-whole scale.

Because of intervallic symmetry, there are only three diminished scales. Other diminished scales, with varying names, can be formed by starting on a different note of one of the three basic diminished scales illustrated in Figure 13-6. Here, you see C, C-sharp, and D diminished scales. If you were to keep building scales chromatically, the next scale would be D-sharp diminished. However, if you remember that D-sharp is the same as E-flat, all you need to do is begin on the third scale degree of the C diminished scale. If you do this, you will have the D-sharp (or E-flat) diminished scale. Again, the symmetrical nature of these scales makes this all possible.

How do you use the diminished scale? As you might imagine, diminished scales can be used on diminished chords. For example, a C diminished scale can be used on a C diminished chord. However, in jazz they are mainly used over dominant seven/flat nine chords and dominant seven/sharp nine chords. For instance, you saw it used in measures five and six of "Jaco Lives." In short, you can use a diminished scale on these types of altered dominant chords because diminished chords are really the same as dominant seven chords with a flat nine. In this case, simply use the half-whole version of the diminished scale beginning on the note name of the flat/sharp nine chord (as in using G half-whole over a G7♭9 chord).

Chapter 14

Creating Your Own Bass Lines

Creating bass lines can be a daunting task. However, if you draw from all of the musical elements you've already learned, building a bass line is simply a matter of putting together the pieces. This chapter will help you to combine the information you've learned so far in this book so that you may create logical, appropriate, and unique bass lines. Additionally, some new tricks and musical devices are given to you so that your bass lines sound as smart as the ones professionals construct.

14

Understanding Song Structures

When creating your own bass line, you have to know where you are going. You must know what the next note and chord will be before you play it, although instinct often makes this more of a subconscious decision. Besides knowing what's next in the short term, you also have to know what's going to happen overall in the song. This structure of a tune is also called the *song form.*

Song form is often associated with letters. Each new section of a song begins with a different letter in the alphabet. The only exception to this is musical introductions and endings. These are usually not lettered unless they appear in subsequent repetitions of the part. Most songs use repeats. Therefore, you're likely to see the letters reappearing later on and over and over.

The first section is called the A section. Unless a song repeats the same groove, chords, and melody over and over—which can be done effectively— then the next section is labeled the B section, then C, and so on. Some songs only have A and B sections. Having a D section or higher, although not unusual by any means, is less frequent. Unless you are analyzing classical or progressive rock, you are unlikely to venture too far into the alphabet. A typical pattern in any popular form of music is likely to show A and B sections repeated throughout with other letters appearing less frequently.

FACT

Every genre of popular music has certain musical forms that are ubiquitous. For instance, jazz often uses the form AABA, while modern pop music often uses the form ABABCBB although some alterations are always to be expected. The Genesis song "ABACAB" borrowed its title from its own song form, serving as an inside joke among the band members.

Another common way to look at musical structure or form, especially in modern commercial pop music, is to use terms such as *introduction (intro* for short), *verse*, *chorus*, *bridge*, *solo*, and *coda* (which might also be called an *outro*). When someone refers to modern commercial pop, that would usually include modern country hits, modern R & B, some hip-hop, plus modern rock. A tune in these genres will often start with some sort of intro then proceed to the verse, which is normally the section where lyrics are expressed most freely. At about the one-minute mark, give or take a few seconds, you'll usually hear the first chorus. The chorus is the section where the main emotional heft of the song is delivered with maximum impact. Here you often find the title of the song and a more repetitive vocal hook, as well as a lift in overall dynamics (volume). Usually the song then returns to the verse section but with different lyrics and perhaps some modifications or evolution of the arrangement and instrumentation.

After that, the second chorus section is likely to appear, and it's often identical to the first. The second chorus may be repeated twice in a row depending on the chorus's length. Next, usually a brand new section, the bridge, appears. The bridge often completes the song by providing the final emotional, lyrical, melodic, and harmonic content that the song heretofore has not tapped into. For instance, the lyric might offer up some additional, crucial information about the story being sung. Or the emotion of the piece might become more desperate. The bridge might also use an obvious chord that has been held at bay previously or saved just for the bridge. It is not uncommon to even venture into another key altogether—often the relative major or minor—only to find your way back to the original key after the bridge ends.

In most songs, tension and release are exploited for emotional effect. Further, after reaching the summit of the final chorus, you should feel like an interesting emotional tale was narrated through music. Often these final choruses will continue on, repeating over and over until some ending or outro can be devised or until the recording engineer fades the song out gradually.

Through your understanding of the structure of music, you can make better choices all around. First of all, you will know what section comes next. Second, you will be able to create contrasts or specific textures in your bass lines for each section. This is especially important when you are asked to write your own bass lines no matter what the genre.

Writing Pop and Rock Bass Lines

It's essential to express emotions and ideas through your musicianship, if only for your audience's sake. To that end, you have to understand the goals and agenda of each piece of music, in each section, and in each genre. If you're playing a bandmate's composition or a cover tune, you need to get inside the mind of the songwriter in an attempt to comprehend what he is trying to say with the song. Even if it's your own song, you need to think about what you want to say with the tune. This is not always easy to know! This is why the most thoughtful or contemplative musicians are usually the best musicians.

If a bass part is more or less prewritten, it's still important to breathe fresh life into it by playing with the right articulation, technique, emotion, and intent. Plus, nine times out of ten, there is always some room for improvisation or modification of an existing part, as long as you make appropriate changes. With all this in mind, you'll need to consider how and what to play in order to modify a bass part for a song. Overall, in rock, pop, country, and other commercial music styles, the bass is almost never out front. Instead, it usually plays a supporting role. However, that doesn't mean that the bass lines have to be tedious or dull.

Minimalism and Modern Pop

A minimalist approach can help the commercial bassist play simple but fresh and interesting bass lines. Minimalism is a form of music that stresses chordal or melodic repetiton and a less-is-more approach. By using very slight variation, minimalist music can evolve but only within very limited parameters. In a modern context, dance/electronica, funk, and hip-hop have been greatly influenced by this reconception of what a melody is. For the bassist, it's important to become comfortable with, and inspired by, the mere simplicity and parsimony of a bass line; this can be a superb complement to technical expertise and virtuosity.

FIGURE 14–1 gives you a glimpse of what minimalism is all about. Notice the two-note bass line in the verse that uses syncopation to achieve a funky feel. In the chorus, there is only one note used to underpin several different

FIGURE 14–1.

Verse and chorus using a minimalist approach

chords. This is not an uncommon bass line in modern commercial music. These repetitive figures could also be thought of as ostinatos. Additionally, the chorus bass line employs a pedal effect.

Although **FIGURE 14–1** uses a funk rock example, these minimalist techniques are also used to varying degrees in all forms of modern bass line construction. Another interesting technique that you can use—one that augments the possibilities of pop genres—is the use of alternate bass notes. This was also employed in **FIGURE 14–1**. Although bassists usually play only the root note of the chord for extended periods, a thoughtful bassist can also experiment with emphasizing different notes pulled out of the given chord. For instance, instead of hanging on the root note of a C chord, try playing the major third, or E. Even a simple progression can be made more interesting through the use of alternate roots. **FIGURE 14–2** illustrates this where I and IV chords are used. Notice how by selecting just the right mix of alternate and regular chord roots you can create an ascending line that really adds to the drama of an otherwise very predictable and drab chord progression.

Try mixing up these techniques with some of the bass line concepts you learned in previous chapters to see how far you have come in your understanding of modern pop bass styles. First, learn the written line in **FIGURE 14–3**, then experiment with your own bass lines using all that you've learned so far in this book!

FIGURE 14–2.
Alternate bass
notes on a I–IV
progression

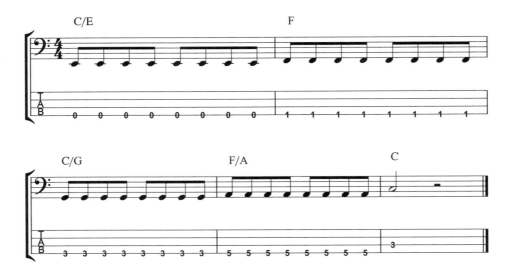

At this point you should be feeling pretty good about using the tools you've learned throughout this book to compose your own professional sounding bass lines. Dig deep and never give up on trying to do something new and original. As long as it sounds good, and your intuition tells you you're on the right track, you're making progress.

Writing Latin Bass Lines

When it comes to other styles, such as contemporary Latin, there are fewer rules and regulations confining your style to traditional approaches. As in modern pop styles, there is more and more cross-pollination from one style to the next. Although most modern Latin electric bass players combine all the styles of Latin music together, they might also pull ideas and techniques from jazz, funk, R & B, pop, and hip-hop. Just as radio, film, television, and the Internet have exposed people from different cultures to each other's way of life, musical styles have broadened and expanded over the last hundred years. In many respects, this is due to the same forms of media listed above. Consequently, the world has become smaller, and this has led to some really interesting hybrid forms of music.

FIGURE 14–3. Sixteen-bar modern pop chord progression with bass line

TRACK 44

There is really so much to appreciate regarding Latin-influenced music. Take a look at **FIGURE 14–4**. Here you'll mix a variety of different Latin grooves together. It can sometimes be challenging to switch from one groove to the next, so be meticulous in your approach. Also, don't forget to count the rhythms. In this figure, you'll see a samba mixed with Afro-Cuban and soca grooves.

Notice that by using a different groove in short spurts you are able to achieve a more songlike sound. In a sense, this is a technique for writing Latin bass lines so that each section of the song is set off or differentiated

FIGURE 14-4. Using a combination of Latin grooves

TRACK 45

from the others. Try to make up your own combination of Latin grooves, something completely different, over these chord changes using the various Latin grooves you learned earlier in the book.

As stated previously, it's common to hear interesting hybrids of Latin, jazz, pop, and funk being played by bands today. What about mixing funk and jazz fusion with some spicy salsa? Why not? **FIGURE 14–5** does just that.

FIGURE 14–5. Latin jazz fusion

TRACK 46

Now you are ready to start your musical journey in South America and borrow from Brazil. Try a soft and mellow pop tune, not unlike something Nora Jones might perform, with some imported bossa nova bass lines.

When blending pop with other styles it's important to find balance. So that the tune does not sound overtly Brazilian, the bass line in **FIGURE 14–6** tones down the root-fifth idea in favor of a simpler root-root approach. Some alternate bass notes are also employed.

FIGURE 14–6. Singer-songwriter pop with bossa nova bass

TRACK 47

Writing Blues Bass Lines

There are so many varieties of jazz and blues that it can be difficult to know where to start when writing bass lines in either of these genres. Part of this is due to the incredible amount of freedom allowed in both styles (especially in jazz music). Therefore, when playing these styles you should think about the unique elements of each piece of music.

When it comes to blues, you have to know what type of blues groove you're playing. Is it a funky blues or a shuffle? Is it a jazzy blues or a slow, soul-searching blues? You also need to know if it's a minor blues or a major blues. The answers to these questions dictate your approach. In fact, you should first ask yourself these questions—and be able to answer them—before you hit the first downbeat.

One of the most enjoyable types of blues to write a bass line for is a slow, swampy blues. Part of the fun is the minimalism that can be employed in your approach. In this case, having a deep, full bass tone also helps to capture the feel of the music. Start by playing some long and full quarter notes in a walking style, then throw in some triplet rhythms, especially leading into beat one of any measure. Occasionally use some swing eighth notes just to add another layer of groove. **FIGURE 14–7** shows how this is done. Give it a try and then try out your own slow-groove blues using these rhythmic devices.

FIGURE 14–7. Slow-groove blues

TRACK 48

Another possibility for a blues line is to use alternate bass notes instead of roots on beat one of some measures. Try playing the third or the fifth, or even the seventh, where you'd normally play a root.

ALERT!

When using alternate bass notes on a walking pattern in blues be careful not to overdo it; otherwise, you might confuse the listener or you might throw your bandmates off. Remember, the main job of the bassist is to play roots. Therefore, use alternate bass notes sparingly so that the listener, and the other musicians, can effortlessly hear the structure of the tune.

FIGURE 14–8 provides some walking lines on a blues progression. Each utilizes some alternate bass notes. As always, see if you can devise your own similar lines.

FIGURE 14–8.

Walking blues lines with alternate bass notes

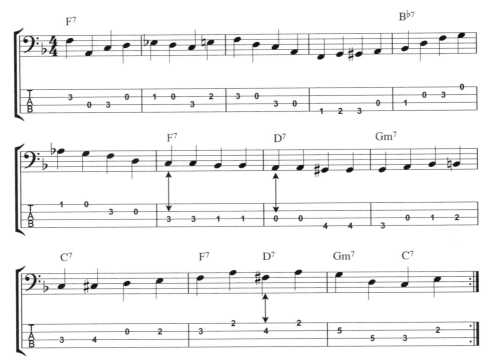

The arrows point to alternate bass notes.

Writing Jazz Bass Lines

When it comes to jazz, you're entering some pretty deep terrain. But don't fear, you've already learned so much! Remember that your best tools for jazz lines are arpeggios, scales, and chromatics. If you fully exploit these tools, you'll have many great options for bass lines at your disposal.

In jazz, angular, unpredictable bass lines can be a plus (unlike in pop where bass lines have to sound fairly safe harmonically). Alternate bass notes are much more common in jazz. Breaking up the rhythm in daring ways is also encouraged. Remember though, it's still important to keep impeccable time, and you must always strive to create a great groove.

One of the ways jazz bassists get that daring sound is by employing *leading tones* and other chromatic devices in seemingly nonharmonic ways. In other words, the chromatics used on a given chord may have more to do with where you'll be next rather than where you are now. Thus, they might appear to conflict with the current chord you're on. Traditionally, a leading tone is the seventh scale degree of the diatonic scale. It is called a leading tone because it sets up or leads into the tonic with great emotional necessity. The leading tone is also the major third of the V chord. In Chapter 17 you will see the connection between the leading tone and the V chord. For now, simply recognize that the leading tone is a powerful precursor or catalyst to the tonic.

In jazz, the leading tone may appear a half step below the tonic of the chord—just like a traditional leading tone—or a half step above the tonic of the chord. Again, the reasons for this will become apparent in later chapters. Nevertheless, using leading tones in jazz as a stepping stone to a chord root creates the same emotional urgency as previously mentioned. Since most jazz walking lines are based on quarter notes, this leading tone will appear mostly on beat four. As for beats two and three, additional chromatics can be used to preface the leading tone and its subsequent root. By studying and playing **FIGURE 14–9**, this should become easier to understand.

FIGURE 14–9.
Using leading tones and chromatics above and below the root

Of course, this idea needs to be fully integrated into what you have already learned about walking bass lines in jazz. In **FIGURE 14–10** you will combine together many of the jazz concepts you've learned so far. In this musical example, you will play a walking bass line comprised of leading tones, scales, arpeggios, chromatics, and alternate bass notes.

FIGURE 14–10. Putting walking bass lines together with all you've learned

TRACK 49

Chapter 15

Learning Tools

Students have a wide range of learning tools available to them. Learning tools can't do the work for you, but there are many products on the market that really do help you to learn music faster and with more retention. Since technology is always changing and improving, this chapter will not go into detail about the latest gizmos. Instead, it will give you a general idea of the tools and accessories that are likely to grow, develop, and remain vital to music education.

15

The Metronome

As you now know, the bass plays an integral role in setting and maintaining the tempo. In order to develop rock solid timing, you'll want to practice with a metronome daily.

A metronome is a compact, plastic box that creates an electronic beep or clicking sound. A flashing light(s) usually accompanies the beep. Moreover, the beeps and the lights are perfectly synced. When you first play with a metronome, you may think it's out of time. This is because you have yet to develop a good internal clock. However, the more you play with a metronome, the better your timing will become.

There are many brands of metronomes on the market, and prices range from around twenty dollars to well over a hundred bucks. Some of these companies include Korg, Yamaha, Qwik Time, Seiko, Wittner, Franz, Boss, and Exacto. You can now also download click tracks from the Internet. Lastly, drum machines can serve as a fancy metronome. For example, you might enjoy playing with a "phat" drum groove instead of a monotonous click.

The best metronomes on the market are ones that can be turned up loudly and that come with an earphone jack. Pocket metronomes cannot be turned up loudly and are of little use for bass players. The classic Dr. Beat DB-66 metronome and the updated Dr. Beat DB-90 metronome offer the most bang for your buck.

ALERT!

Whatever metronome you use, stay far away from manual, wind-up, or pendulum metronomes. These are completely obsolete and their timing is not exact. A metronome that keeps questionable time could actually hurt your playing, so only use electronic metronomes.

The Dr. Beat DB-66 metronome offers many features. One of those is a dual light. One light is designated for beat one only; the second light pulsates on the remaining beats in the measure. In 4/4, beat one blinks on the left side of the metronome while beats two, three, and four blink on the right side of the metronome. The Dr. Beat can also play multiple rhythms.

In other words, you can add eighth notes, sixteenth notes, or triplets to the mix simply by turning up the volume on the individual sliders. Furthermore, the Dr. Beat offers a wide range of tempo and meter choices. It also features a tap function. The tap function allows you to set the tempo by tapping the speed you desire. A digital readout will tell you what tempo you are tapping. You can then set the metronome accordingly. Lastly, to save on the cost of batteries, the Dr. Beat comes with an AC adapter. This is really helpful since metronomes tend to use up batteries quickly.

Setting the Metronome

There are many ways to set a metronome. If you're in 4/4, you may want to set the metronome to represent quarter notes or downbeats. However, if you're playing at a fast pace, you may want to set the metronome to represent half notes. If you're having trouble syncing up with the metronome, you might set it to eighth or sixteenth notes (depending on your tempo). This will help you keep the beat easier. Most importantly, make sure the clicks and lights fit the time signature of the music. The loudest click should always represent beat one.

FACT

If you set the metronome to sixty, there will be sixty clicks played per minute. In other words, the metronome will be clicking seconds. The higher the number the more clicks per minute. The lower the number the fewer clicks per minute.

Sometimes students set the metronome then forget to listen to it as they play. Don't let this be you. The metronome must click in time with your rhythms. Otherwise, it's serving no purpose. If you have a difficult time playing in sync with the metronome don't stress. You'll get it. That's what practice is for. However, don't just ignore the metronome. **FIGURE 15–1** shows a series of rhythms in 4/4 with metronome pulses indicated above the staff. In this time signature, the metronome is usually set to play quarter notes. Notice how the quarter notes line up with the downbeats of each rhythm.

FIGURE 15–1.

Playing with a
metronome

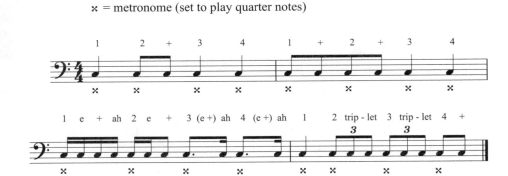

Tap the rhythms to **FIGURE 15–1** slowly on your lap. You may also clap them if the tempo is not too fast. Also, make sure you count the rhythms out loud as you tap. You will tap more precisely when you count aloud.

Measuring Your Progress

During your practice routine, set the metronome at a moderate to slow speed. If you're playing too fast, you probably will play sloppy, inarticulate rhythms. On the other hand, if you're playing too slow, you may find that you rush through all of the rhythms. Stick with moderate, attainable tempos at first.

Once you find a comfortable speed, don't be in a rush to increase the tempo. Instead, maintain this pace until your playing feels natural and flowing. When you're ready to move on, increase the tempo in slow increments. As you do this, you may want to keep a written log of the tempo increases you've made.

Your practice log should be used to evaluate your progress. (For more on practicing, see Chapter 19.) Over the course of many days you will start to see a pattern emerge. If you're making improvements, your tempos will increase at a slow but steady rate. However, if you're attempting to play speeds that are beyond your ability, the metronome log may show erratic tempo shifts or no clear progress.

Each day you may find that you have to back up from the previous day's top speed then build from there. This is natural, and it probably means that you just aren't warmed up yet. Also, sooner or later you will come up against a wall and you will not be able to play any faster. Finding your wall is a good thing. It allows you to set realistic and definite goals.

Your goal should not necessarily be to play fast. Bassists must also be able to play slow, funky grooves. As you practice, try slowing the tempo down gradually. You'll find that the slower you play the harder it is to play accurately. This is because the slower you go the more space there is between notes.

Practicing with a metronome can be exasperating, so you might be tempted to turn it off when you practice. When this urge strikes you resist! Developing the ability to play with a metronome is a sign of skillful bass playing, so make this one of your main objectives.

Music Writing Software

With Sibelius, Notion, or Finale score writing software, you can now format your written music to look as clean and articulate as the published materials that come out of mainstream publishing companies. No longer do you have to scribble tunes out by hand on staff paper. Score writing software has now made it possible for musicians and music students to format their music with the same kind of accurateness and professional appearance as a top-notch publishing house.

Both Finale and Sibelius contain sheet music templates. With a click of the mouse, you can choose a variety of staff paper. For example, you can select a jazz quartet staff, a salsa band staff, or create your own. Once you choose your staff, you then select a key and time signature. You may also indicate tempo. After this, you can begin inputting notes either through a keypad, keyboard shortcuts, or a MIDI hookup. When inputting notes through an interface, you can play a keyboard, or a MIDI bass, and the notes will appear on the page.

FACT

As of this writing, you still have to edit notes inputted through MIDI hookups so that your music is readable. However, MIDI inputting continues to get more and more intelligent with every upgrade. It's reasonable to assume that this software will eventually become quite efficient and accurate.

Sibelius, Notion, and Finale also offer excellent sound libraries to play back your music. This helps you to proofread with your ears as well as your eyes. No longer do you have to imagine what your tune will sound like, and you can also catch mistakes easier. There's no telling how far this software will evolve, so get involved with it now. It can help you to better communicate your tunes to others with greater intelligibility. It can also help you to better learn about the basics of writing standard notation and tablature.

Band-in-a-Box

Band-in-a-Box is used to accompany a soloist, and it's an excellent tool for those practicing improvisation. To use it, all you need to do is install the software onto your computer, type in some chords, choose a style of music to play, and begin soloing. When indicating chords, you can write simple triads or complex chords with all kinds of harmonic extensions (for example, F7♯9). Band-in-a-Box does the rest for you. Depending on the style of music you choose, Band-in-a-Box will interpret the music and voice these chords appropriately. From jazz to rock, blues to Latin, Band-in-a-Box plays it all.

Band-in-a-Box is especially helpful when learning how to improvise in jazz and blues styles. You might start by trying a basic blues. To do this, enter I, IV, and V chords into Band-in-a-Box. Once you've done this, practice soloing over these chords at different tempos. If you're more advanced, try soloing over jazzy blues chord changes or tunes from the so-called Great American Songbook.

Like a metronome, Band-in-a-Box will keep you honest. This software plays with complete accuracy, so you will know if you're dragging or rushing or if you're attempting a speed or tune that is beyond your abilities. More than anything, Band-in-a-Box will help you find out what your strengths and weaknesses are as a soloist. If you're a beginner, you will also get a feel for what it's like to actually perform with musicians. However, keep in mind that real musicians are not machines who play as perfectly and smoothly as Band-in-a-Box.

Home Recording

Home recording has made remarkable changes over the last twenty-five years or so. Prior to the digital age, most home recording was done on multitrack cassette decks. Tascam's Portastudio was especially popular in the early 1980s. These machines allowed people to record up to eight tracks, but the sound quality could not compete with the two-inch tape, reel-to-reel, and console setups found in professional studios.

By the mid 1980s, digital audio tape (DAT) recorders became a feasible home-recording option, but this was limited to recording live to two tracks. In 1991, the Alesis digital audio tape (ADAT) was introduced, which allowed aficionados to record up to eight tracks onto Super VHS magnetic tape. Despite the promise of this technology, home-recording engineers still needed to bounce tracks down or synchronize machines together if they wanted to record more than eight tracks.

If you're new to home recording, try Apple's GarageBand. GarageBand allows you to build loops from their collection of instrument samples. You can also record your own instruments by using an interface or a microphone. Further, GarageBand has lots of fun reverbs, EQ settings, and user-friendly editing options.

Today, home computers are used to create recordings that sound top-notch. Also, there are virtually no limits to the amount of tracks you can use. If you have good ears, reasonable computer skills, ample workspace, and a lot of patience, you can record your tunes at home. To get started, all you need is a Mac or PC and a digital audio workstation (DAW) such as Pro

Tools, Nuendo, Cubase, Logic, Digital Performer, or Sonar. Next, you need an audio/midi interface. You might also consider an array of quality plug-ins (reverbs, compressors, and equalizers). If you plan on recording acoustic or live instruments, you will also need some microphones. Once you know how to use this technology, you can engineer and produce your own music.

Recording as an Educational Tool

Documenting your work is extremely educational. Past generations of music students had few opportunities to record their playing, but today, the sky's the limit! If you record yourself regularly, you can better measure your progress, and this will help you to better structure your practice routine. In a sense, you can be your own teacher.

How does this work? Through recordings, you can listen to performances after the fact then judge your work. Once you remove yourself from the mechanics of music making you will be able to listen with a more objective ear. In other words, you will be able to hear yourself as others hear you. This is an invaluable tool, especially if you do not take private lessons. It's hard to critique your playing in the heat of the moment. However, if you go back and listen to what you played after the fact, you will be able to assess your music with more insight and clarity.

When listening to recordings of yourself what should you listen for?

- **Time keeping.** If you find that you are not keeping steady time, spend more time with a metronome.
- **Rhythmical accuracy.** Are your rhythms clean and fluid? Do you play with intent and confidence? If not, again, practice with a metronome. If you're having a lot of problems with rhythm, buy a beginner drum method book—yes, a drum method book—and practice tapping or clapping rhythms. This will help you to better understand rhythms. It may also help you to create tighter grooves with the drummer in your band.
- **Tone.** Are you creating an attractive and expressive sound on the bass? If not, think about how you're plucking or picking the strings

and how you're depressing each string. Also, ask yourself if your bass is in good shape. Have you had a setup recently? Is it out of tune?

- **Appropriateness.** Think about how well you're gelling with the other musicians in the band, particularly the drummer and the singer or soloist. Are you too loud? Too soft? Too busy? To spare? Are you driving the music or do you sound soggy and logy? Does the music feel good or does it feel stiff, uninviting, or mechanical? Feel is everything!

- **Proper bass lines and improvisation.** Proper or good bass lines are not easy to devise. Hopefully by now this book has set you on the right path. The goal is to properly fill out the lower end of the band's sound without getting in the way of the lead singer or the soloist. If you're in a situation where you improvise, are you playing thoughtful solos? What about your note choice? Do you make lots of errors when you solo or do you play lines that fit well over the chord changes? There is nothing worse than sketchy improvisation. It's important to use your ear and your knowledge of music theory to discriminate between right and wrong notes. Also, it's important to know the difference between hip notes and passable notes. Obviously, some of this is subjective. The best way to learn about note choice is to listen to and internalize the bass playing of the masters. Will you play a wonky note on occasion? Yes. However, if wrong notes are commonplace, you need to rethink your approach to improvisation and make soloing or improvised bass lines a bigger priority during practice time.

Chapter 16

Reading Charts and Lead Sheets

In Chapter 16, you will learn how to read and interpret charts and lead sheets. These two items are essentially the same. Both are musical skeletons. Unlike classical repertoire, charts and lead sheets do not include every single note that will be played by the performer. It's up to the musician to flesh out the chart. Charts typically consist of chord symbols and a notated melody. Sometimes lyrics are also included. Other musical symbols and terms may be used, and key rhythmical patterns or ostinatos may also appear in a chart.

Straight Talk about Charts

One of the most frightening things about being a bass player is the prospect of having a piece of music thrown in front of you and having to play it cold. This is called *sight-reading*, which means to play a written piece of music without any real practice or preparation. Some musicians are better than others at this. But any way you dice it, sight-reading is an invaluable skill. No matter what style of music you play, you should develop some capacity for reading a chart on the fly. At first this task can be frustrating. However, with a little practice and know-how, you will get the hang of it.

ALERT!

Bass charts can vary depending on the type of music played and the tendencies and preferences of the person writing the chart. In general, your success with charts rests on your ability to read and interpret musical shorthand.

There is always a nomenclature associated with any specialized pursuit. This is also the case with music where there is a substantial lexicon of musical terms that you must learn. Throughout this book you've been introduced to a moderate dose of these terms. However, there are still many more to learn. In fact, there are whole dictionaries dedicated to musical vocabulary. *The New Grove Dictionary of Music and Musicians* is the most famous of these publications.

Brace yourself for this next piece of information: Since this chapter focuses on chart reading, you will not see tablature. Tab is never included in a chart. Given this, you should start weaning yourself off of tab. Tab is used primarily as a learning tool for beginner and intermediate-level guitarists and bassists. It is never—or very rarely—used in real-life playing situations. If you plan to play professionally or even semiprofessionally, you will, however, need to know how to read standard notation and charts. Making the transition is not easy, but you can do it!

Terms and Symbols Used in Charts

Because Western music is primarily derived from European classical music, most of the terms used in music are foreign to American speakers. Italy was the epicenter of the Renaissance in art and music, and the majority of the musical terms musicians use today sprang from that era. By studying and familiarizing yourself with these terms, you will be able to converse with other musicians in an intelligible way and, most importantly, be able to follow the musical direction dictated in a chart.

If you're going to be a real musician, you should purchase a music dictionary. It's a helpful reference guide to the terms you'll inevitably encounter when reading music of any kind. Even if you don't purchase a full unabridged version, there are smaller pocket-sized versions that will cover the majority of terms you'll need to know.

Despite this, you're still going to need to memorize a lot of musical terms since they come up so often. *The Everything® Bass Guitar Book* can't hope to catalog all the terms you'll need to know and memorize. However, here is a starter list of musical terms:

- **Tempo:** the speed or pulse of the music. Sometimes exact tempos are shown in the top left corner of a chart. Other times, tempo is indicated using terms such as *adagio* or *allegro*.
- **Adagio:** slowly
- **Andante:** a little faster than adagio, often described as a walking speed
- **Moderato:** medium or moderate speed
- **Allegro:** a lively or quick pace often described as cheerful. Extremely fast tempos are usually notated as *vivace*, *presto*, or even *prestissimo*.

Although you should know traditional tempo markings such as adagio, andante, moderato, and allegro, they are used less and less in contemporary chart writing. Instead, simpler language is often used, such as slow bossa, fast bop, or pop ballad. These terms indicate both tempo and feel.

- **Ritardando or rallentando:** these terms are interchangeable and refer to a gradual slowing of tempo, usually written as the abbreviations *rit.* or *rall.*
- **Accelerando:** gradual increase in tempo, usually written as the abbreviation *accel.*
- **A tempo:** return to the original or first tempo.

The following terms are related to expression and articulation:

- **Pianissimo (pp):** very soft
- **Piano (p):** soft; a notch louder than pianissimo
- **Mezzo piano (mp):** moderately soft; louder than piano but softer than mezzo forte.
- **Mezzo forte (mf):** medium loud; usually a natural, unforced volume that exists in the middle of the dynamic spectrum
- **Forte (f):** loudly
- **Fortissimo (ff):** very loud
- **Accents:** an accent tells you to emphasize a specific note or notes through a sudden increase in volume. There are two main types of accents. Both are seen as carets in the music. A caret that points upward is a strong or particularly forceful accent. Other terms such as *sforzando* (*sfz*) and *fortepiano* (*fp*) also tell you to give a note an extra emphasis or dynamic punch.
- **Crescendo:** gradual increase in volume, denoted by a widening hairpin symbol or the abbreviation *cresc.*
- **Diminuendo or decrescendo:** interchangeable terms that refer to a gradual decrease in volume, denoted by a narrowing hairpin symbol or the abbreviations *cresc.* and *dim.*
- **Fermata:** hold or freeze on a note or chord indefinitely; sometimes called a bird's eye

The following terms relate to navigation:

- **First/second ending:** at the end of a section in a chart you may see two endings. In this case, the first ending always includes a repeat.

After you take the repeat, you will play your way through the music again and take the second ending.

- **D.C. al fine:** repeat to the beginning and end where you see the word *fine*, which means "end" in Italian.
- **D.S. al coda:** repeat to the sign then jump to the coda when indicated. You will end on the coda.

Many of these terms are used, and labeled, in the condensed sample chart shown in **FIGURE 16–1**. (It would be impossible to include every term in one chart.) This sample uses the more difficult D.S. al coda. In the real world, you might also see D.C. al coda and D.S. al fine. Also, you'll see hash marks (/ / / /) used in most of these measures. This tells you to keep time playing the basic rhythm or ostinato that was given to you.

Once you have a basic command of note reading and you can implement the essential musical terms listed above, you are ready to read down a chart. Any written piece of music has, as you know, a beginning, an end, and hopefully some musical variety in the middle. But beyond these vague notions of what is going on in any given piece of music there are common patterns, signs, and structures that appear and reappear in most pieces of music. You've already dealt with chord symbols, key signatures, time signatures, and repeats, which are probably the most ubiquitous structures of all.

How to Read a Chart

One of the most important things to do when you read a chart, especially if you're sight-reading, is to look the chart over from top to bottom before attempting to play it. First look at the time signature. Are you in 4/4 or another time signature? Next, look at the tempo. Are you playing slow or fast or somewhere in between? Is there a metronome marking or some other indication of tempo, such as allegro or moderato? Look for directions regarding style and feel. Does it tell you "bossa nova," "bebop," or "hard rock"?

The next step is to look for the key signature. Are there sharps or flats? Are you in C major, B minor, or E-flat major? Also, are there strange accidentals

FIGURE 16–1.

Condensed
sample chart

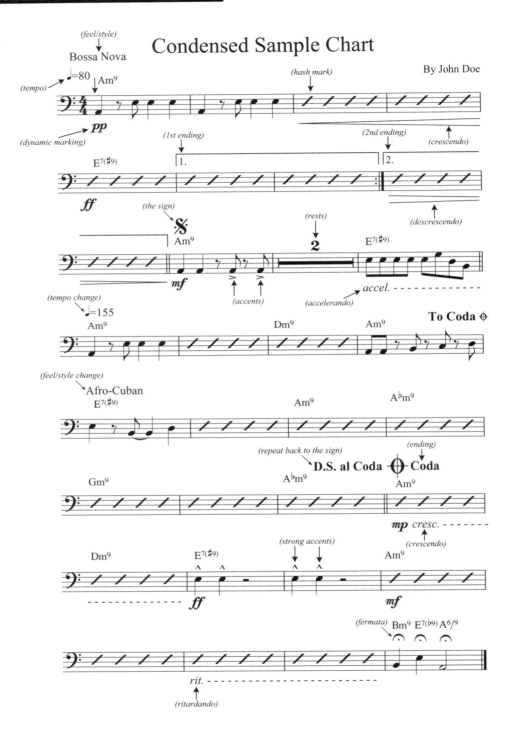

that pop up in the music? After that, look at the chart's basic structure or road map. Are there repeats or endings to follow? Are there any D.S.s or D.C.s, codas, or any other special directions that you need to take note of? Lastly, look for terms that designate expression and articulation. Are there dynamics (*p*, *mf*, *ff*) or accents?

As if this wasn't enough, it's also important to scan for solos. If solos exist, a good chart will tell you. Most importantly, do you have a solo? If so, review the chord changes that you'll be improvising over. Take a look at the overall anatomy of the chart. Can you spot A, B, and C sections? If you can, you will get a better sense of the song's overarching structure. Lastly, check out any written notations that look knotty or gruesomely complex. If you can, run through these passages a couple times before the tune actually starts. If you have time, practice playing your bass lines over the chord changes.

The most important thing to keep in perspective is the overall quality of your performance. It doesn't matter all that much if you make a slight error. Chances are the audience won't notice. What really matters is keeping up and not getting lost. If you do get off in the chart, try to get back on by using your ears. Above all else, play with confidence, intent, and leadership.

Improvising Within a Chart

Although you might see bass charts with every note written out, it is more common to see chord changes or a mix of chord changes and written out bass lines. When a chart is made up of chords, with or without a melody, it is often referred to as a lead sheet. Lead sheets are condensations of a given piece of music. Often, lead sheets are used to represent popular tunes. When reading a lead sheet, it's assumed that you will not attempt to duplicate a given arrangement or recording note for note. Rather, you will recreate the overall feel or gist of the tune. Lead sheets are used extensively in jazz where the performers improvise over the melody and chord changes of a tune. One thing's for sure, lead sheets encourage—indeed require—interpretation and spontaneity.

If you need to come up with an improvised bass line, first try to determine the basic style. Ask yourself if it is a rock tune, a Latin tune, a funk tune, a swing tune, a country tune, or a blues shuffle. Within these styles there are further refinements. If it is a rock tune, is it a hard rock song or a pop ditty? If it is a funk tune, is it a Motown style or modern slap-bass style? Luckily, you'll often find the style listed at the top left of the chart.

Once you know what style you're playing, your creative impulses and musical habits need to kick in. You'll have to be able to turn chord changes into compelling bass lines and licks on the spot! If you don't know where to begin, start simple. Remember to listen to the drummer, rhythm section, and the entire band in order to lock into the tempo and groove. As the tune progresses, you can always evolve your approach to include fancier lines and licks. But at first, keep it simple. Also, if you're toggling between written lines and improvised chord sections, you need to stay alert, otherwise you will miss sudden shifts or changes in the music.

If you play a solo in the chart, you need to create licks that set themselves apart from your bass lines or ostinato patterns. To do this, you'll often want to venture up the neck into the higher range of the instrument. Also, when you solo in the higher register, listeners will be able to hear your ideas more clearly.

Improvising over a chart is difficult because you are reading music as you play. When you are sight-reading and attempting a solo, it is not necessary to turn every chord change into a new melodic line or lick. Instead, play through the changes. By emphasizing the key center and the important chords, you can simplify the harmonic content that you are basing your solo on. Often, one or two scales are sufficient in partnership with the chords. **FIGURE 16–2** shows how this may be done. The chords are complex, but a one-scale-fits-all approach actually works. With some practice and experience, you will develop the ability to simplify the chords in a chart until you find the harmonic and melodic common denominators.

FIGURE 16-2.

Simplifying complex chord changes in a chart

Tempo Changes

Another challenge when reading a chart or lead sheet centers on tempo changes. Tempos are usually consistent within a given piece of music; however, it is not uncommon to find changes during some tunes. Having a tempo change during a song presents certain problems, especially when that change is communicated to you through a written chart. Usually the change will be written exactly as it occurs. If you are lucky, a metronome marking may indicate an exact value. This will be written with a quarter note placed above the staff with an equal sign and a numerical value. Theoretically, if the tempo is increased to twice as fast, the new beats per minute (BPM) value will require multiplying the initial numerical value by two. For example, if you are at 60 BPMs and the music asks you to play "double time," you will now play at 120 BPMs.

Unfortunately, tempo indicators are not always that precise. Since traditional (Italian) tempo marking have a range of approximate values, it can be difficult to pin down exactly how fast any tempo should be let alone how fast or slow the new section should be. This is just something that you have to get used to.

Tempo is often best viewed as a relative concept. In other words, if you are to move from one tempo to another, the second tempo may be based on the initial tempo in a relative way. It can still be exactly twice as fast, but you may not have an absolute value for either tempo. Furthermore, many tempo changes are fairly arbitrary. In some tunes, you simply get faster, as in the change from moderato to allegro, or slower, as in the change from andante to adagio. In these cases, you must use your best judgment.

If you are making these changes as a band, it helps to follow the drummer. You may also designate one musician to be the leader. Sometimes this person even conducts the change (similar to classical music conducting).

This is not commonplace though. Usually the leader will communicate the tempo or feel change through exaggerated body language and playing gestures.

The two most common types of tempo change keep the relationship between the two different tempos at a fixed, predictable ratio. As mentioned just previously, "double time" just means to play twice as fast. Likewise, "half time" means to play half the speed. In order to pull these tempo shifts off with accuracy, you must conceive of them properly. When making such changes, your knowledge of note values and note relationships must guide you into the next tempo.

For example, if you have "double time" indicated in the chart, simply turn your current quarter-note value into eighth notes. Since eighth notes are twice as fast as quarter notes to begin with, you can use them as the basis for reformulating your tempo. For half time, move in the opposite direction and turn quarter notes into half notes. Since half notes are half the speed (or twice the length) of your initial quarter-note pulse, they provide the perfect basis for reformulating your new quarter note speed.

Changing the Feel

Sometimes a chart or lead sheet will ask you to play a double time or half time "feel." In this case, the word "feel" changes the way the music is perceived but not the actual tempo. Instead of literally shifting the tempo to twice or half as fast, the chart may ask you to play a groove that implies double time or half time. If this seems confusing, don't worry—it's not that complicated.

Here's how it works: The main thing to keep in mind is that the measures and chords will go by at the exact same rate as before. In other words, the note values do not shift. Also, the tempo remains consistent, but the feel or groove is made to seem twice as fast or half as fast. In essence, you are pretending to go into double time or half time by playing twice the speed or half the speed as requested. Again, the chordal movement, or rate of change, remains unaffected and untouched.

Another way to conceive of this is to double or halve your note values while keeping your tempo consistent. For instance, if you are playing quarter notes over the changes, now play eighth notes to create a double-time feel. If you are playing quarter notes and you are going to do a half-time feel, you'll need to play half notes. **FIGURES 16–3** and **16–4** show how this is done. Notice that the chord changes, tempo, and measures are consistent while the rhythm is doubled or halved accordingly.

FIGURE 16–3.
Double-time
feel

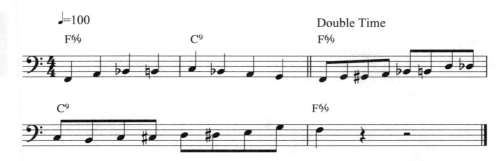

FIGURE 16–4.
Half-time feel

Chapter 17
Advanced Theory

You might have heard the adage, "If you are not growing as a musician, you're dying." This means if you're not advancing your knowledge and skills, then you're on your way to becoming over the hill, rusty, or obsolete. One of the endless musical enigmas revolves around understanding the full scope of harmonic and melodic complexity, which has evolved through many centuries of composition and improvisation. Through the study of classical and jazz theory, you can unlock these secrets and expand your skills as a bassist indefinitely.

Extended Harmony: The Role of Sevenths

If you want to become an advanced bassist, studying jazz theory is a must. Believe it or not, jazz theory can spice up your rock and pop playing too. For example, a close inspection of some of the Beatles' most interesting tunes reveals the use of chord progressions and tricks of the trade often associated with jazz and classical music. In many ways, that's why their songs are so compelling. Furthermore, if you study harmonically sophisticated music (such as jazz) you will simply be more informed and knowledgeable as a musician. The more informed you are, the easier it will be to play any style of music.

One of the things that jazz is known for is its use of extended harmony. More than just about any other form of music, jazz stretches harmonic complexity to the max. Extended harmonies revolve around adding notes, in stacked thirds, beyond the simple triad. These extensions might be sevenths, ninths, elevenths, and/or thirteenths. They add color to the music while simultaneously assigning a deeper function to a chord. So, extensions change or augment the emotive content of a chord while they also help to delineate the specific harmonic role of that chord.

FACT

When utilizing extended harmonies, there are both aesthetic and functional considerations. The aesthetic aspect relates to individual chord colors while the functional aspect refers to how a chord is used contextually, that is, the relationship between chords. In short, the chord progression reveals the quality and function of each chord as well as enhancing a basic aesthetic component.

At first it may be difficult to differentiate between each kind of chord extension, but through careful listening and dedicated application you can learn to hear their differences. In time, you will also learn how these various extensions may be used. Start with sevenths.

Sevenths were introduced in Chapter 7, and it might be helpful to review that chapter before tackling this section. There are two completely different kinds of sevenths: major sevenths and minor sevenths. Major sevenths are spelled out as maj7, Δ⁷, maj⁷, or ma⁷. Minor sevenths may be used on minor seventh chords or major dominant seventh chords and are spelled out as min7, m⁷, mi⁷, or even with a dash (-7). If you're moving progressively through this book, you've seen some of these symbols already.

Aesthetically speaking, a maj7 chord has a sweet sound and is patently pretty. Maj7 assigns a function generally associated with I or IV chords in a major key, though they may also accompany minor chords. In this case, they exude the classic sound of film noir. Think of the eerie chords you often hear in black-and-white detective movies!

Dominant seventh chords—written like D7, F♯7, and B7—are commonly attached to both major and minor triads. When used as an extension of a major chord, they are generally bluesy sounding. When used in most chord progressions where blues is not an emphasis, the functional aspect of the chord comes to the fore and the dominant seventh, on a major triad, expresses itself as a V7 chord. Since V chords are powerfully drawn to a subsequent I chord, they often are followed by a progression to the I. On the other hand, when the dominant seventh is attached to a minor triad, the chord has a quintessentially jazzy and hip sound. Although in modern music this chord is often seen as an i chord in a minor key, it implies modal diatonicism (Dorian) and is most commonly associated with the functionality of the ii chord in a major key.

In order to internalize these sounds and understand these functions better, try the exercises in **FIGURES 17–1** to **17–6**. In **FIGURE 17–1**, you'll review the different combinations of seventh chords as arpeggios. In **FIGURES 17–2** to **17–5**, you'll get a chance to construct bass lines using all four combinations of sevenths. Lastly, in **FIGURE 17–6**, you will see how three of the most common seventh chords are employed in a ii–V–I progression.

FIGURE 17–1.
Seventh
chord review

Listen carefully to each arpeggio. Pause between each to appreciate their distinct sound and composition.

FIGURE 17–2.
Major triads with major sevenths over a Gmaj7

Notice the multiple symbols that may be used to represent a G major 7 chord.

FIGURE 17–3.
Major triads with dominant sevenths over a G7

FIGURE 17–4.
Minor triads with major sevenths over a Gm(maj7)

FIGURE 17–5.
Minor triads with dominant sevenths over a Gm7

FIGURE 17–6.
A ii–V–I progression using sevenths

Higher Extensions and Upper Structures

The next note in the order of extended harmonies is the ninth. Ninths are construed three different ways. First, there is the major (or natural) ninth. This is used in conjunction with any of the sevenths mentioned previously. Basically, the ninth supports and amplifies the color of whatever seventh is used over the triad (major or minor). Sometimes the ninth is used minus the seventh. In this case the ninth has a less jazzy sound and instead evokes a more pop-oriented feeling. This usage of the ninth is also called *add 2*. The other ways that you'll see a ninth configured are as a sharp nine (#9) or a flat nine (♭9). These varieties of ninths are only used in conjunction with major chords with dominant sevenths. So, in effect, they are only used as *dominant* functions. In other words, they are used as a V7#9 or a V7♭9, especially in minor keys (keys where the i is minor). In fact, if you intend to add a ninth extension in a minor key, it generally is a sharp or flat nine, not a major or natural nine. Superscript numerals can also be used to denote ninth extensions.

Sharp and flat nines are functionally equivalent. This means that both attach themselves interchangeably to dominant seventh chords in their functional role as V chords, often in a minor key. Color-wise, however, sharp and flat nines both have different aesthetical qualities. The sharp nine tends to be edgier, bluesier, and meaner sounding. On the other hand, the flat nine tends to be sweeter and prettier, albeit melancholy. Ballads may be more appropriate for flat nines while funkier, more Afrocentric jazz (like 1960s-era John Coltrane or Miles Davis) tends to demand the energy and unsettled feel of a sharp nine. See **FIGURE 17–7** where both sharp and flat nines are employed as V chords going to minor i and major I chords.

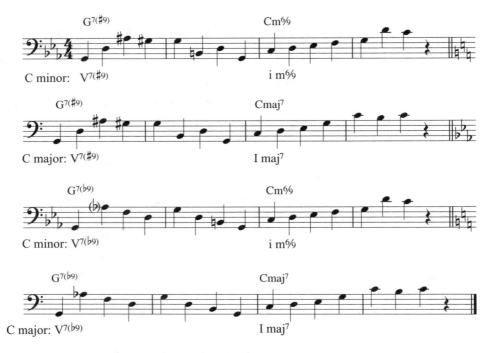

FIGURE 17–7.
Sharp and flat nines followed by minor i and major I chords

Notice the key changes and chord functions!

Elevenths and Thirteenths

The eleventh is an interesting upper extension that colors the lower end of a chord in diverse, perhaps opposite, ways. There are two types of eleventh chords: natural elevenths (C11) and sharp elevenths (C7#11). The natural eleventh is synonymous with the suspended fourth (sus4). In fact, both notes are the same except that the eleventh may be voiced an octave higher. When in use, the natural eleventh usually supersedes the third, especially when the chord is major. In this case, the major third is omitted and the chord ceases to actually be defined as major or minor (although it often replaces and resolves as C7/11 going to C7). In most situations, the natural eleventh is used on V chord functions, and it is almost identical to a suspension except that it may have additional color due to the way it's supported by the seventh and ninth. The natural eleventh goes well with just about any chord except for major seventh chords, to which it is anathema.

The other variety of eleventh is the sharp eleventh (#11). This extension attaches to virtually any chord type, though it is less commonly seen attached to minor chords. When attached to major seventh chords (usually I or IV chords), the sharp eleventh has an otherworldly, consonant yet transcendent, sound. When attached to dominant seventh chords (often V7 chords), the sharp eleventh challenges the ear and sounds funky, soulful, and bluesy.

Check out the suspended quality of the natural eleventh and the otherworldly quality of the sharp eleventh in **FIGURES 17–8** and **17–9**.

FIGURE 17–8.
Natural eleventh chords as suspensions over dominant and minor seventh chords

FIGURE 17–9.
Sharp eleventh chords used with major and dominant seventh chords

The last and highest extension is a thirteenth. This extension works well over any type of chord. It is the same note as a sixth, though an octave higher. There are both natural thirteenths and flatted thirteenths. While the natural thirteenth is used with just about any chord quality, the flatted thirteenth is used almost exclusively with dominant seventh chords that employ flat or sharp nines. Flat thirteens are equivalent to augmented fifths except that they presuppose the support of the ninths and/or elevens situated below.

Thirteenths seem to have no readily discernable sound. Instead, they add complexity and harmonic fulfillment to whatever chord they are paired up with.

When chords contain extensions going as far as the elevenths or thirteenths, those last three or four notes are often called *upper structures*. If you examine the last three or four notes of any of these combinations of chords, you'll notice that these last notes often form recognizable chords in and of themselves.

For instance, a C7/9/♯11/13 has a D, F♯, and an A as its top notes. These notes also make up a D-major triad. Next, try a C7/9/11. This chord contains the top notes B♭, D, and F. These are the same notes used in a B♭-major triad. Your solos and licks will sound hyper-hip if you know how to apply this knowledge. One way to implement it is to use simple arpeggios to dance around the upper structures of extended chords. **FIGURE 17–10** provides an example of this.

FIGURE 17–10.
Upper structures as simple triads

Advanced Chord Functions

Consider the dilemma of modern biology. We were taught in school that there are certain immutable species that are unique and separate entities. But at some point we learn that life is more complex than that. Now we know that species evolve, mutate, interbreed, and hybridize, and that the concept of a species is, in some cases, more a matter of classification than some hard, eternal truth. There is a corollary in music. Music students start out thinking that keys never change, that the function of a chord is clear and neat and that things are either one thing or another. The deepest truth is that, often, especially in more challenging music, these apparent absolutes are not absolute at all. Instead, they are relative.

Music, as you know, happens in time and space. As melodies, rhythms, and harmonies evolve through time, their context—past, present, and future—all impinge on each other locally and globally. For instance, a V chord sets up the expectation of resolution to a I chord. But what if that V chord goes to another V chord? Subsequently, what if the old I chord, acting now as a V, resolves to the chord that is its I chord? **FIGURE 17–11** illustrates this knotty concept through notation.

FIGURE 17–11.
Harmonic
sleight of
hand

So that you can better focus on the chord functions extensions have *not* been added to the Roman numerals.

Perhaps the most powerful force in Western harmony is the energy created and released between and by the movement between the V or V7 chord and the I chord. By adding a little twist, such as topping the I with a dominant seventh, you can create long chains of endlessly unresolved V7–I7 progressions. Why? Because now the I7 is a dominant seventh, just like the V^7 that preceded it. It might just as well be viewed as a V7 too. In **FIGURE 17–12**, this concept is taken to its limit. You can see that every chord is now the V7 of the next, which is the V7 of the next, and so on, ad infinitum. This is the kind of trickery that some composers devise to transport their composition (and the listener) to new key centers. All you have to do to stop this musical madness is to finally decide not to add a dominant seventh and simply make camp at a newly desired key center.

Here's another musical trick: turn the minor ii chord into a major II. You can also add a minor (dominant) seventh to the chord as well. If you arpeggiate a D7–G7–Cmaj7 chord progression, you'll probably recognize it as something you've heard many times. But why does this sound so neat? Again, it's because the II7 chord is not really a II chord as much as it is the V7 of the primary V^7. In this case, the primary V7 chord is a G7. Music theorists

FIGURE 17–12.

Dominant chords can create a musical hall of mirrors

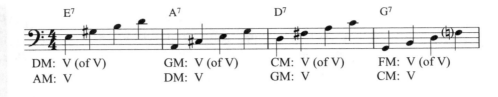

DM: V (of V)   GM: V (of V)   CM: V (of V)   FM: V (of V)
AM: V   DM: V   GM: V   CM: V

BbM: V (of V)   V   I
FM: V

Note: Keys are often indicated with the letter of the key and a upper case "M" for major and a lower case "m" for minor. No minor keys are used in this example.

call this musical mirror a V of V. A slash mark is used to denote this, and it's written as *V/V*. This is similar to the previous harmonic hall of mirrors.

So, the same force that draws I and V7 chords together draws V7/V7 chords together. The only difference is that, instead, the pull happens to be between V chords. The general title given to this dominant-to-dominant, or V/V, relationship is *secondary dominance*. In the example described above, the D7 functions as the secondary dominant in the key of C major. This is because D7 is the V7 of G7. This will all become clearer as you get a chance to experiment with these chords.

Using Chord Substitutions

In a sense, when employing the rules of secondary dominance, or V/V, you are substituting one chord for another. In this case, the V/V substitutes for the normal ii chord. When this is voluntary and done at will—as in jazz music—it is called a *chord substitution*. Jazz players do this regularly and habitually.

There are many kinds of harmonic substitutions in music. One of the easiest ways to figure out some of these substitutions is to experiment with alternate bass notes. One of the common strategies is to see if a chord a third above, a third below, or a fifth below creates a pleasant alternative. These intervals can either be major or minor thirds, or perfect or diminished fifths. You want to look for notes that are common to both chords. For instance, if you are given a C-major chord and you want to substitute something else, consider Emin, Amin7, Fmaj7, or F#min7♭5. These four substitutions all share at least two of the same notes. But be careful. When substituting chords you often must maintain the major or minor chord tonality or the chord substitution(s) may not work. In the C-major example, the major third of Cmaj is E. In all the viable substitutions above, the E remains inviolate and untouched.

Another strategy for substitution that can be very exciting is to use any chord that fits the melody of the tune. For instance, if a G is played in the melody over the given Cmin chord, you might try an E♭maj7 or an A♭maj7 since these both complement the melody G note. Of course, there are other options as well, too many to list here. Sometimes these kinds of substitutions can be functional or nonfunctional, depending on your taste.

One of the most famous substitutions, and one that bassists regularly use, is something called *tritone substitution*. Tritone substitution is a substitution that occurs on any dominant seventh chord but works best when the given chord is functioning as a V7 chord. This includes secondary dominant chords as well.

ALERT!

In the blues, you may see dominant seventh chords that are not acting as V7 chord substitutions. For example, in the blues, I7 chords really are I chord functions. The same is true for IV7 chords. Needless to say, be careful with substitutions on these particular dominant sevenths.

To perform tritone substitution on any dominant seventh chord, simply find the dominant seventh chord that is a tritone (an augmented fourth or diminished fifth) away. For example, if you have a G7 chord and you wish to perform tritone substitution on it, you would play a C#7. Remember, a tritone is exactly six half steps (or frets) above or below your given root.

The reason that tritone substitution works so well is that the third and seventh tones in both the original and substituted chord are exactly the same. Looking at the G7 and C#7 chords, both share a B and an F for their major thirds and dominant sevenths. As a bassist, you can exploit this opportunity by actually performing tritone substitution at will even if the other members in the band are not necessarily performing it. Try substituting the dominant seventh chords in **FIGURE 17–13** as you see fit. It's time to improvise!

FIGURE 17–13.
Tritone substitution ad lib

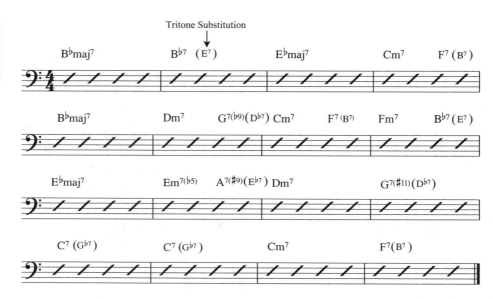

Possible tritone substitutions are shown in parentheses. Never attempt to use tritone sub. on major or minor seventh chords.

Chord Insertion

It's expected that you will use secondary dominance (V/V chords) and tritone substitution in modern jazz. In fact, exploiting dominant chords is the name of the game! So far, you have learned how to use V/V chords to spice up your playing. You also learned how to create some different types of chord substitutions, the most common of which is tritone substitution. The final trick is to squeeze these chords into real music, which is called *chord insertion*.

In order to fit your inserted chord into a chart, you have to shorten some of the other chords' durations. Start by inserting dominant chords. Any dominant chord can have its V chord placed in front of it. **FIGURE 17–14** shows

FIGURE 17–14.

Inserting dominant chords

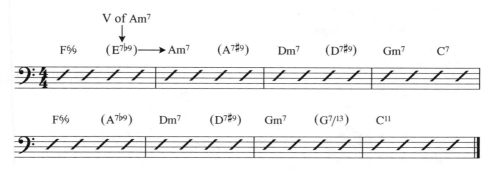

Each chord in parentheses is the "V" chord insertion of the chord that follows.

how this is done. As you improvise a bass line over these chords, make sure that you hit the roots at the right time (downbeats).

This is where it gets exciting. As previously stated, harmony can be a complex hall of mirrors. As you know, dominant chords can be preceded by their dominants. Additionally, you can precede a dominant chord with its ii chord, or you can swap out dominant chords with tritone substitutions. In **FIGURE 17–15**, you'll get to experiment with all of this. Try applying this information to jazzy tunes or to charts you may be working on with a teacher.

FIGURE 17–15.

Inserting the V7, the ii of V7, and the tritone substitution

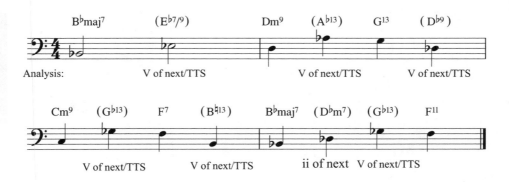

TTS indicates tritone substitution. "Next" refers to the next chord.
Parentheses indicate insertion.

Chapter 18

Minor Keys and Additional Theory

By this point you have encountered some pretty heavy material. You should feel proud of what you've accomplished. There are only a few more basic items that you need to investigate in order to be truly ready for the musical world as a bassist. In this chapter you'll receive some additional tools and theory that you'll need if you want to convincingly play jazz, Latin, and more advanced styles of rock and pop. Ultimately, this material will help you develop greater command of your instrument and music in general.

Minor Keys and Functions

Throughout this book you've dealt with minor keys and chords in a general way. Many of the same basic principles apply to minor keys as they do to major keys. The first step in understanding minor tonality is to look at the key signature. Remember, key signatures tell you how many sharps or flats are in the music. Also, keep in mind that every minor key has a relative major key (that is, a major key that shares the same set of sharps or flats). If you play white notes—together with pitch alterations delineated in the key signature—you will be playing the notes that make up a natural minor and relative major scale (see Chapter 4).

Since this chapter focuses on minor keys, you may disregard the relative major for the moment. The next step in utilizing the natural minor scale is to turn the scale into basic triads, then seventh chords, and so on. Just as in major keys, these chords constitute the chord functions in a given minor key. **FIGURE 18–1** illustrates the outcome of this process.

FIGURE 18–1.
Chord functions derived from the natural minor scale with sevenths

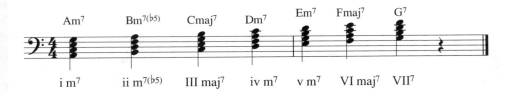

You'd expect these harmonic derivations from the natural minor scale to be the last word on minor chord functionality; however, they are only the beginning. To be fair, the chords spelled out in **FIGURE 18–1** may be used as the "proper" functions in a minor key. From Renaissance music to Bob Marley reggae classics, these natural minor chord functions have provided the harmonic basis for many songs and compositions. However, more often than not, life in a minor key is more convoluted and complex.

Just what is it about a minor key that makes it different and more complex than a major key?

The most notable difference between major and minor keys and chord functions is how the V chord and vii chord are altered in a minor key. In minor keys, the V chord becomes major (that is, the third of the chord is raised). The vii chord is also rooted on the major seventh scale degree (more akin to the harmonic minor than to the natural minor) rather than the minor seventh degree. When the vii chord is rooted on the major seventh it becomes diminished (now, vii dim or viio). In minor keys, these alterations require the use of accidentals.

By making the V chord major in a minor key and by rooting the vii° chord on the major seventh scale degree, the natural minor scale, seen before as our guiding principle, has been diminished in importance. This violation of the natural minor—in favor of alterations to the chords themselves—is accomplished by the use of accidentals. **FIGURE 18–2** shows this adjustment. The harmonic seventh on the i chord is often adjusted in a likewise manner, so here you'll also raise it to the major seventh or leading tone.

FIGURE 18–2.
Common chord functions in a minor key with sevenths

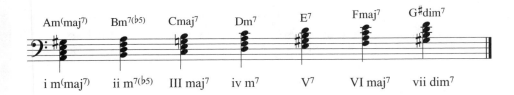

But what's really going on here? What's happening is that the seventh scale degree is being raised for the V7 and vii dim7 chords. This is exactly like the modification made to the natural minor scale when modifying it to become the harmonic minor scale. This is a great way to conceive of it. The only caveat here is that, in reality, it is probably the scale that comes second, meaning that it is not the scale that dictates to the chord how it should be modified; rather, it is the other way around. In other words, the outcome of the harmonic pressure to modify the V chord from minor to major so that it has the same dominant sound that the V chord has in a major key. Because of this, the natural minor scale gradually morphed to accommodate the raised seventh scale degree. Eventually the harmonic minor scale became an important underpinning in minor keys.

Minor ii–V–i Progressions

Before moving on, you'll need to try a couple chord progressions using the minor chord functions just described. First, try a sample chord progression using the natural functions derived from the natural minor scale. **FIGURE 18–3** gives you a chance to try this using arpeggios. After reading the given bass line, feel free to mix up the pattern of notes, and positions used to generate them, in an improvisatory way. Likewise, **FIGURE 18–4** gives you the opportunity to outline chord functions in minor that use raised seventh scale degrees. Remember, when you do this, you are making the V chord major and the vii° chord diminished. (Diminished is, again, a minor triad with a flatted fifth. B-D-F is one example.) After reading the bass line provided, improvise using a mix of the broken chord notes.

Like in major keys, the ii–V–i is still an important and fundamental type chord progression. Here it often takes the form of a ii min7(♭5) –V7–i min(maj7). Sometimes, a dominant seventh or a major sixth may be substituted for the major sevenths on the i chord. When adding ninths, on the ii chord the ninth is often, surprisingly, major. It's surprising because the major

FIGURE 18–3.
Chord progression using natural minor functions

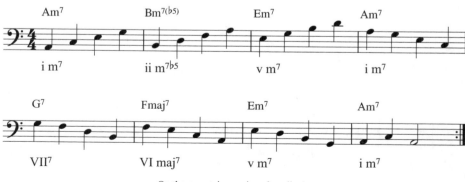

On the repeat, improvise a bass line!

FIGURE 18–4.
Chord
progression
using minor
functions with
raised seven

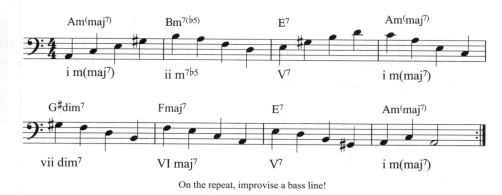

On the repeat, improvise a bass line!

ninth violates the minor third of the key itself. Nonetheless, this major ninth tends to sound consonant. However, you may also use a minor ninth (or ♭9) on the ii chord as well. This is especially common in scalar usage. When adding a ninth to the V chord in a minor key, it is almost always sharped or flatted. Rarely, the V chord, in this context, might take a major or natural ninth. A famous example of this rarity is in the classic Gershwin tune "Summertime" from the 1935 opera *Porgy and Bess*. As far as the i chord is concerned, if a ninth is applied, it is always a major or natural ninth.

Altered Chords and Tritone Substitution Revisited

The act of sharping or flatting a ninth on a dominant seventh chord is often referred to as *altering* a chord. It is also typical to have an augmented fifth (more properly referred to as a flatted thirteenth). When a chord has these elements, it is in the classic form of an altered chord. Thus, when you're in a minor key, the V chord should normally be altered since this is more common and generally preferred with V chords in minor settings.

When a chord is altered, an interesting equality is produced between the chord tones of the altered chord and the chord tones of its potential tritone substitution. The only tones not identical here are the roots and fifths of each possible chord. However, when the sharp nine is utilized their specific roles become inverted. This only occurs when the altered chord is compared with its unaltered tritone substitution.

For example, a Gb7 altered (or Alt.) contains B♭, F♭, (better known as E), A, and D. This voicing excludes the root and fifth. Its unaltered tritone substitute, C7/9/13, contains an E, B♭, D, and A. Again, this excludes the root and the fifth. As you can see, the notes that make up these specific chord tones are the same. This continues when you use a flat nine (♭9) instead of a sharp nine (♯9), though the flat nine of C7/9/13 equals the fifth of the G♭7. If a sharp eleven (♯11) is present in the C7/9/13, that note (F♯) is enharmonically equivalent to the root of the G♭7.

All in all, what you should take away from this is that these chords are essentially interchangeable, and it is merely the root note, as a matter of emphasis, that makes the two options—one a given and one a substitute— two versions of the same underlying reality.

This situation affects your bass lines in two ways. First, it gives you the option of playing the actual dominant chord or the tritone substitute at will, at least in jazz music anyway. In the simplest language possible, this means that, when inserting dominant chords, you can play a proper fifth above the next destination chord or a half step (always one fret) above that same next chord. Second, this freedom allows you to walk through a series of ii–V or ii–V–i(I) progressions in a descending manner, which produces a smooth chromatic transition between each chord. **FIGURE 18–5** shows you how this can be done tastefully.

FIGURE 18–5.
A succession of ii–V and ii–V–i(I) progressions using descending bass lines

Possible Minor ii–V–i Scales

Besides hitting the roots at the right time, the main occupation of bassists is to create inspired melodies or bass lines. You know that roots, arpeggios (broken chords), and scales all play a huge role in the development of these lines. You've looked at complex arpeggios and roots (including root substitutions), but you haven't yet taken a truly thorough survey of the appropriate scales to use with these complex chords.

First, take a look at the scales that are consonant with minor ii–V–i progressions. Start with the ii chord. So far, you know that the ii chord is minor with a flatted fifth, a dominant seventh, and often a major ninth. If you extend the chord all the way to the thirteenth, even observing the i's natural minor scale, you'll get a natural eleven and a flatted thirteen. These notes, when added to the ii chord, produce a scale most commonly recognized as a melodic minor scale. The problem is that it is not the melodic minor of the given chord but, rather, the melodic minor scale whose root and name is found a minor third above. When this is the case, the term *mode* is most often applied.

ALERT!

You've encountered modes throughout this book. However, in cases where the modes are not derived from major, diatonic scales (like Ionian or Dorian), these modes may be called new names depending on the starting point of the scale. This occurs only when you start on a scale degree other than the tonic. For example, when using the melodic minor as a mode, you might say, "the sixth, second, or third mode of the melodic minor." It all depends on the starting pitch.

When looking at the notes derived from the extended ii chord (but using primarily a major ninth), you will see that a scale is formed. The scale associated with this chord is a melodic minor. Again, it is not the melodic minor scale of the ii chord itself. Instead, it is the melodic minor scale of the pitch located a minor third above the ii chord.

There is another way to look at this too. On the sixth scale degree of this melodic minor, you'll find the actual root of the given ii chord. For example, if you have a Dm7♭5 as your ii chord, you can use the melodic minor scale located a minor third above that chord. In this case, that scale is an F melodic minor. Moreover, when playing a standard F melodic minor (F, G, A♭, B♭, C, D, E, F), you will see that its sixth scale degree (D) is equal to the root of the original ii chord. That means that you are officially playing the sixth mode of the melodic minor scale. The only difference is that you do not play the notes from F to F (as in the standard melodic minor scale). Instead you're playing the notes from D to D. In short, if you play the F melodic minor scale moving from D to D over a Dm7♭5 or ii chord, you are playing the sixth mode of the F melodic minor scale.

Admittedly, the formal name of the proper scale may not really make a difference if you are soloing since you can simply play the F melodic minor inverted or excepted in any manner you choose. However, it may become important when starting your bass *line* from the root of the given ii chord and ascending to the next chord (presumably the V).

However, in many cases, bassists choose to ascend to the V chord without observing the major second that is part of the sixth mode of the melodic minor scale. Instead, they simply follow the key signature (which produces a minor second) when ascending the bass line. Funny enough, each bass line option may produce an equally compelling result when walking to the V chord, yet this may not be true in solo situations. When soloing, the melodic minor is usually the preferred scale. **FIGURE 18–6** lets you hear both options and decide for yourself.

At the end of the day, it is usually okay to use the notes from the key's natural minor over the ii chord. This is a usable but more basic approach. It's also great to use the modal melodic minor. Not sure what to use? Ultimately, trust your ears. Thankfully, these two scales really do exhaust the list of what to play over ii chords in a minor key.

FIGURE 18–6.
Walking to the V chord using the natural minor and modal melodic minor

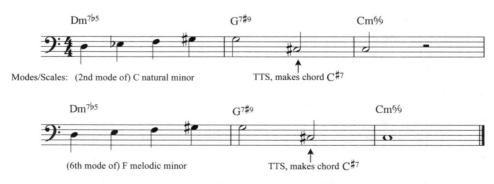

FIGURE 18–7.
F melodic minor and the sixth mode of F melodic minor

"D" is the sixth scale degree.

F melodic minor   Sixth mode of F melodic minor.

FACT

When the natural minor and melodic minor scales begin on different scale degrees, other names are sometimes used. For instance, the natural minor beginning on the second scale degree, or ii chord, may also be called a *second mode natural minor scale*, a *seventh mode Locrian scale*, or an "*Aeolian flat two*." Regarding scales names, it's really just a matter of taste.

For the rest of the chords in the minor ii–V–i series, the formula is simpler. When it comes to the altered V chord, which is common in minor keys, the formula is simple: play the melodic minor one half step (one fret) above the name of the V chord itself. It doesn't matter if the chord uses a flat nine or sharp nine. This melodic minor (also known as the super Locrian or "diminished whole tone") works equally well on sharp nine or flatted nine V chords. There are a few other options, however.

When using a V chord that contains a flat nine and a natural thirteen, the optimal scale is a diminished (octatonic) scale. In this case, the diminished scale must move in a half-step-to-whole-step manner. (This applies to both major and minor keys.) A less common but very emotionally compelling version of a V chord is found in major keys more than in minor ones, yet it is actually related more closely to the minor key. This is known as the V7♭9(sus4) or phrygian chord.

When navigating over this chord, you will play the melodic minor scale located a whole step below the letter name of this distinctive V chord. This scale is officially known as the phrygian sharp six. In the extremely rare case of having a natural ninth but an augmented fifth, you can use a scale known as the whole tone scale. This scale simply ascends in whole steps only (every other fret). **FIGURE 18–8** shows an example of each scale paired up with the appropriate chord symbol.

Lastly, it's time to dissect the minor i chord. The most consonant scale you can use here is the melodic minor of its very own name. That makes it the easiest chord in the minor key pantheon. In fact, you may be pleased to know that there is no modal melodic minor to even deal with! Chord symbols such as Cmin(maj7), Cm6/9, and C-, all will work well with C melodic minor scale as their accompaniment. The most common changeup here is the regular minor seventh chord. In this case, the Dorian mode of the chord usually works best. This mode is the same as the natural minor of the

FIGURE 18–8.
Four types of altered V chords

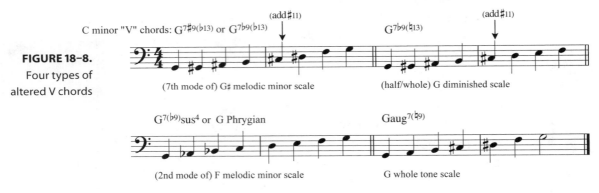

Note: there are generally *several* other names for each scale.

FIGURE 18–9.
Various minor i chords with accompanying scales

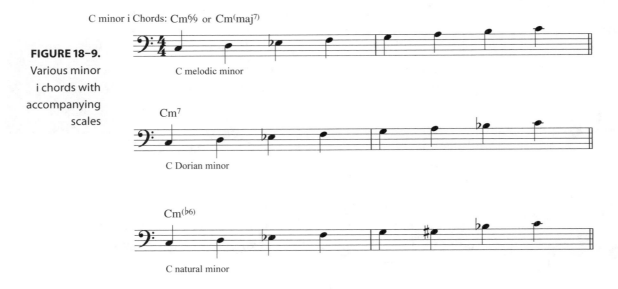

chord itself but with a raised sixth scale degree. Another much less common chord is a minor i with a flat sixth (for example, Am ♭6). Here the natural minor of the chord name works extremely well. **FIGURE 18–9** illuminates these possibilities.

Applying What You Know

You know a lot by now! Some of the material, especially in the last two chapters, may seem extremely convoluted and theoretical—or just plain hard! But don't worry; you really do know just about all you need to know about theory. In all fairness, there are many more topics that one could study. Especially missing is a study of traditional classical music theory. However, the electric bass is not a classical instrument; therefore, advanced classical theory would not impact your playing all that much. If you'd like to check out how this theory is implemented by bassists, simply listen to modern jazz. The topics discussed here are universal. In fact, all jazz bassists build lines and solos using this harmonic information. Some of the theory you learned about in Chapters 17 and 18 may seem arcane and boring to you. However, when it comes to constructing bass lines, these really are important concepts. For instance, if you are playing Latin, salsa, traditional country, thoughtful pop, avant-garde, funk, fusion, jam band music, or progressive rock, you will probably, sooner or later, need to deal with these kinds of chord progressions. It's better to deal with them with poise rather than to fall on your face because you've reached the limits of your musical literacy.

In this final section of the chapter, you'll see a thirty-two bar jazz etude to both read and improvise over. When you solo, be sure to apply your knowledge of chord functions, arpeggios, and scales. Start out slow and practice this etude over and over. This may be the beginning of your first serious attempt to play like a real jazz bassist! You can do it!

FIGURE 18–10. Jazz etude "Be Bop Drop"

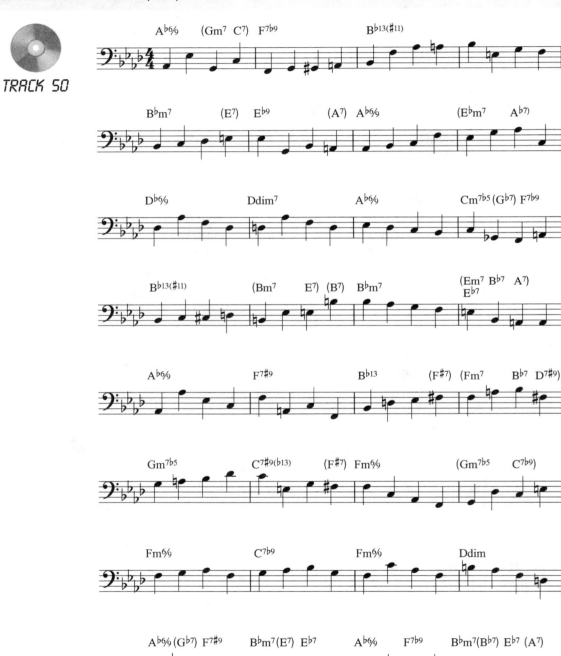

TRACK 50

Chapter 19
Practice Tips

Now that you've learned about the nuts and bolts of bass playing, it's time to learn some general tips. To play the bass—or any instrument—you need to develop a daily practice regimen. This chapter will give you some tips designed to keep you organized, productive, and focused. Learning the bass requires both discipline and motivation. It is not enough to just jam each day. Instead, you need to set goals and meet them. This chapter will show you how to commit to a practice routine and stay structured day to day.

Setting Goals

There is no magic fairy dust that can make you a great bass player. In the end, it comes down to hard work and organizational skills. The best way to excel on any instrument is to set short-, medium-, and long-term goals. This will ensure progress and productivity.

Unfortunately, some musicians only set short-term goals, like learning how to play a specific bass line or how to play a particular song. Others only think about far off, distant goals like being able to play as good as, say, Paul McCartney or Geddy Lee. It's good to have musical heroes and it's okay to aspire to greatness; however, lofty long-term goals should be tempered by more realistic short- and medium-term goals.

Before you even play one note, sit down and make a comprehensive list of short-, medium-, and long-term objectives. Then design a practice routine based around these goals. Don't know where to start? That's okay! The following are some questions to consider when setting goals.

- **What are my current skills?** List them under subheadings. You may want to create the following categories: reading skills, improvisatory skills, stylistic skills, technical skills, creative skills.
- **What do I play well?** Think about your strengths and weaknesses.
- **What needs work?** Again, consider your strengths and weaknesses.
- **What style(s) of music do I want to learn?** Be as specific as possible. Most teachers encourage students to learn general concepts and skills. However, it's okay to say to yourself, "I want to learn modern rock" or "I want to learn slap bass." It's important to determine what you want out of music.
- **What style(s) of music should I learn in order to expand my musical horizons?** For example, rock bassists who have no intention of becoming jazz players often study jazz in order to learn more about harmony and improvisation. Foreign styles of music can expose you to new, creative possibilities.
- **What style(s) of music and/or artists should I avoid?** This is a tough question but one that is important to consider. Generally, you should be open to all genres of music, but be careful not to emulate questionable musicians. Remember, anybody can make a CD these days.

How do you define what is bad? As you become musically educated your discerning ear will answer this question for you.

Defining Goals

What are short-, medium-, and long-term goals? A short-term goal is something that can be achieved in a day, a week, or, at most, a month. A medium-term goal might take you many months or even a few years to achieve. Long-term goals fall into the category of dreams and aspirations. These are lifetime goals. If anything, long-term goals may be the hardest to settle on. If you're not sure what you want out of music, remain patient and observant and focus on short- and medium-term goals for now.

ALERT!

Many musicians aspire to be rock stars, but very few musicians actually achieve rock stardom. Those who do get famous often find that being a rock star is not as romantic and glorious as they thought it would be. Avoid vanity goals, which are based on ego and conceit. It's better to pursue musical excellence.

Music instructors can help you to define goals, but ultimately you should decide what is best for you. No two people are alike; therefore, no cookie-cutter list of objectives can be applied to you. Reflect on music and decide what it means to you. If you're not sure, listen to a variety of artists for inspiration (and not just bass players). Find out who motivates or excites you to want to pick up the bass and play.

Getting Started

If you don't know where to begin, first outline your short- and medium-term goals. If you're a beginner, your short- and medium-term goals should be to learn the basics of playing the bass. In general, all beginner and inter-mediate-level instrumentalists should focus on:

- Technical studies (practicing scales, arpeggios, and other mechanical exercises)
- Music theory (understanding harmony, melody, and rhythm)
- Reading and writing music (understanding notation and, for guitarists and bassists, tablature. Also, you should know how to read charts and lead sheets.)
- Ear training (the ability to identify intervals, chord types, and rhythms through listening)
- Improvisation (Contrary to traditional, classical instruction, all musicians should learn how to improvise on their instruments. This is especially true of those who play instruments commonly found in rock, pop, country, jazz, and Latin bands. The bass is a key instrument in all of these styles.)

Once you understand the basics of music, you will be educated enough to start making informed decisions about your musical future. As you hone your skills, you will likely redefine your goals. This is okay. It is even encouraged. As you progress, you will need to update and revise your objectives because new possibilities will come into view.

Using Your Time Wisely

In order to make the most of your practice time you will need to be organized. Many students waste time in the practice room. Logging time is not enough. Instead, you should focus on how you spend your time. You can practice eight hours a day and get nothing done or you can practice one hour a day and make great strides. It all comes down to efficiency. To make the most of your time, think about the following questions:

- How well do you prioritize?
- How well do you concentrate?
- Can you focus on one task for at least ten minutes?
- Do you stay on task or do you get sidetracked easily?
- Do you work in a logical, step-by-step fashion?
- Is your practice routine based around short-, medium-, and long-term goals?

If you're excellent at prioritizing, concentrating, staying on task, and working in a logical, step-by-step manner, then you're right on track. However, if you're unorganized and scatterbrained, then you will need to change your approach. The best and simplest way to stay on track is to create a to-do list before you practice. Once you've created this list, make sure you adhere to it.

Efficiency in the Practice Room

Don't waste your time in the practice room. Before you even play a note, think about your list of goals, then plan out each practice session in advance. It's also good to create an itemized list (mental lists are okay too, provided you have a keen memory) together with a timetable. The following details a mock one-hour practice session.

1. Review C, F, and G minor scales in various positions. (10 minutes)
2. Begin learning the bass part to "Good Times, Bad Times" by Led Zeppelin. (35 minutes)
3. Practice soloing over a C major blues. (15 minutes)

Notice how there is variety included in the above practice list. If you practice just one item, or just one exercise, your mind could wander. Mix it up to avoid monotony. Most of all, if you schedule your practice time in advance you will spend less time wasting time.

How long should you practice? This is up to you to determine. Some musicians practice four hours a day; others practice only thrity or forty-five minutes. Again, it all depends on your goals. If your goal is just have some fun with music you might only practice a half hour a day. If you want to be the next Stanley Clarke you will need to practice many hours a day. But unless you're a six-year-old child, you should not practice less than half an hour a day; a half hour really is the bare minimum.

Self-Evaluation

In order to practice efficiently, you should ask yourself a series of questions each day. The following questions will help you to evaluate your progress. These are general questions so feel free to revise this list to suit your needs. Also, be specific in your answers and honest in your responses.

- What did I practice yesterday?
- Did I accomplish this task?
- Did I meet my short-term goal(s)?
- Do I need to review or am I ready to move on to something new?

If you feel that you're ready to move on in your studies, ask yourself the following questions:

- What is the next logical step?
- What should I focus on?
- Do I need to revise my short-, medium-, or long-term goals?
- Am I working gradually but steadily toward meeting my goals or have I strayed?

If you've been performing with others, reflect on your most recent experience(s). Ask yourself the following questions:

- How successful was my performance?
- What sounded good?
- What didn't sound so good?
- Am I being realistic about my performance?
- Am I being too hard on myself or not hard enough?
- How should I structure my practice time to make any necessary improvements?
- Was there any constructive criticism given to me during or after my performance? If so, what was it?
- Do I agree with this criticism? If not, why?
- Was I well received by other musicians and listeners? If not, why?
- What can I do to make my playing better the next time I perform?

Asking questions like these will help you to better organize your practice time. This will, in turn, help you to mature as a musician. One word of caution: self-evaluation helps you to better understand your needs and goals, but it should not turn into self-interrogation. The bottom line: strive to maintain a positive, constructive attitude during times of reflection.

Know Thyself

When you evaluate yourself, you are really taking stock of your strengths and weaknesses. Every musician—even the best and brightest—has weaknesses or flaws. For example, some musicians are master improvisers but they can't read music very well. Others can read just about anything but they can't improvise at all.

When it comes to strengths and weaknesses, you have an important choice to make. Do you accept who you are or do you work to overcome a weakness? If your musical vocabulary is limited you should strive to become more skilled and knowledgeable. However, if you're a proficient player, you might accept that there are some things you will just never excel at. You don't have to be brilliant at everything. Some musicians choose to be specialists in one style. As a bassist, you might want to focus on blues, funk, R & B, modern rock, or jazz fusion. It's all up to you.

Through self-evaluation you will gradually define your strengths and weaknesses. The better you understand your musical abilities, the better your playing will get. Make sure you always weigh your strengths and weaknesses against your goals. For example, if you realize that you're poor at reading music, think about how that will affect your goals. If you plan on playing in a funk band then reading music doesn't matter much. However, if you plan on playing bass in a big band, then you will need to get your chart reading together.

"Know thyself" is a quote attributed to the Greek philosopher Socrates. This maxim is not just philosophical flimflam. Self-awareness is important for musical success. The better you understand your strengths, weaknesses, likes, and dislikes, the better your musical journey will be. If you don't take time to understand who you are musically, you will lead a directionless musical life.

A chart outlines a song's meter, structure, and harmonic and melodic content. However, notation is not used exclusively. Instead, charts rely on musical shorthand. To read a chart, you need to be able to interpret chord symbols. See Chapter 16 for more on chart reading.

Taking Lessons

Music is best learned through mentorship, so taking private lessons is highly recommended. It's not easy evaluating yourself. In fact, critiquing your own skills can be a confusing task. Your perceptions are always biased one way or another. This is where a teacher comes in.

Every bassist should take at least a handful of lessons. If you're serious about playing this instrument, it's recommended that you find a qualified teacher and work under his tutelage for months or even years. As you become more advanced, you should study with a variety of teachers. To do this, you may need to travel to different cities or countries. This is also recommended since you may not have all the resources you need in your hometown.

FACT

Music lessons are not just for kids and amateurs. Professional musicians often take lessons from time to time as part of their continuing education. Music instruction doesn't end with a college diploma or a successful performing career. The quest for knowledge and growth should continue indefinitely.

The best musicians are humble about what they know. This is because they realize that there is always something to learn. It's best to always consider yourself a student. Even if you're a professional, it's important to remain open to change and growth. It's arrogant to think that you know absolutely everything.

Self-taught musicians sometimes claim that they don't take lessons because they think a teacher will spoil their individuality or crush their creative spirit. This is an immature attitude and one that will limit your progress. As a student, you may find that there is some advice you reject from your teacher. This is okay, as long as you don't do it out of ignorance. You will stunt your musical growth if you completely reject private instruction because you think that teachers ruin individuality.

Good teachers help you to learn faster and they help you to develop your own style. A teacher will also unlock many mysteries for you. This will allow you to develop at a quicker rate, and you won't spend as much time reinventing the wheel.

Further, if you work with a teacher, you will be able to bounce ideas off of one another, and this alone is invaluable. Most of all, a teacher is a reliable and constructive critic who will help to shape you into a confident musician. Learning to play any instrument can be difficult. Why not let someone help you? It will make the journey a lot less bumpy.

Avoiding Burnout

Burnout is commonplace in music. Why does this happen? Playing an instrument is not easy. It can be very frustrating or even daunting. If you're like most musicians, you will feel good about music on some days and disappointed about music on others. This is normal. The key is to not give in to musical depression. Given the right attitude, music can really enrich your life. It would be a shame to turn your back on the wonders of music just because you're frustrated with something.

Sometimes a practice session, rehearsal, or performance might start to go astray. Don't give up midway through the session. Play every note like you really mean it. Don't get lazy or cynical. Always give it your all. If you feel disappointed at the end of the day, let it go. It's more important to maintain your faith in tomorrow. You can't change the past, but you can learn from it.

When you self-evaluate, make sure that your criticism is productive and your internal dialog is fair and gentle. Instead of saying, "That was awful," say, "I will do better next time." If you make a mistake in a performance admit fault. However, never attack yourself. Sometimes musicians become their own worst enemy. Negativity begets negativity. The more you beat yourself up the more your self-esteem will drop, and soon you will feel totally burned out. If others criticize you, hear them out. Try to learn from their insights. Don't take it personally, even if somebody is coming on a little strong. Understand that most of the criticism you will hear from others will be directed toward your current or most recent performance(s), not your overall abilities or potential. Most of all, try to balance negative reactions with positive reinforcement and always keep your eye on the prize. What is the prize? Growth, perspective, wisdom, and personal satisfaction.

FACT

Successes are delightful and heartwarming, but you learn from defeat also. As strange as it sounds, it can be educational to fail an audition, get a bad review, or get fired from a band. If interpreted properly, these negative experiences will motivate you to improve your playing. You will also develop character, humility, and fortitude.

Chapter 20

What's Next?

This final chapter contains some supplementary information every bass player should know. It contains no-nonsense straight talk about playing in a band, plus it details a system for ranking musicians from amateur to major celebrity. This chapter also gives you an overview of the music business. Further, the following pages contain practical advice on how to guarantee musical growth every day of your life through the triangle of success. All of this is geared toward helping you live up to your full potential as a bassist and as a musical thinker.

Playing in a Band

Playing in a band can be either a rewarding or frustrating experience. It all depends on the circumstance and, most of all, your outlook. If you approach ensemble playing with realistic expectations your life will be enriched. However, if you have lofty goals or an overly idealistic perspective, you may find that playing in a band is frustrating or even downright maddening.

In order to pave the road for success, start by finding like-minded musicians. You will quickly find yourself alienated or even at loggerheads with your band members if you choose the wrong people. One of the best ways to find like-minded musicians is to go see local bands that you like. If you don't know of any local groups, get out there and scope out the scene. Also, jam sessions can provide an opportunity to not only meet other musicians but also to see how well you actually perform with others.

When playing at jam sessions, it's best to avoid showboating. If you show off—in order to prove that you are the best bassist in the room—you will probably make the wrong impression. Instead, keep it simple and focus on the requirements of the music itself. This means playing like a team player. A jam session is a proving ground. However, quality musicians will be looking for taste, style, and appropriateness more than how many notes you can fit into a bar or how many different styles you can represent in one song. More than anything, other musicians look for rock solid grooves in a bassist. In short, they want to feel comfortable soloing or singing overtop.

Once you find players who have similar tastes and goals, work on developing a body of tunes. You may want to write your own material or cowrite songs with others. You also might elect to play covers. Covers are interpretations of other people's music. For example, there are Beatles cover bands, Led Zeppelin cover bands, U2 cover bands, and so on. Most cover bands play a mixture of tunes culled from the songbooks of various artists. In other words, your average rock/pop cover band might play some Beatles, some Rolling Stones, some Eagles, some Billy Joel, some Bruce Springsteen, and so on.

Cover Bands Versus Original Bands

Generally speaking, cover bands make more money than original groups as they play private gatherings such as weddings, bar mitzvahs, holiday parties, and corporate events. Original bands are usually found only on the club scene, and unless you play in a band with a large following, you will not make much money in clubs. In some cases, you may find that you actually lose money because of the pay-to-play syndrome. Because of this, you should think about what your objectives are as a band. As you do this, don't lose track of your personal objectives too.

If your group is interested in music strictly as a hobby, then performing and recording will be extremely rewarding. However, if you're looking to sign with a major record label, tour the globe, and sign autographs after each show, then you could be headed for disappointment. Bottom line: fame is rare in any business.

If you play original music, it is strongly recommended that you draw up a legally binding intraband agreement. This agreement sets down on paper the intellectual property rights for the songs you create. Intraband agreements detail who gets what in the event of a hit single or a lucrative album sale. This means royalties. In general, intraband agreements protect the rights of individual band members.

When playing in any type of band, the best attitude to have is one of careful optimism. You should always work hard to make your dreams a reality. You must also accept the unpredictable nature of the performing arts. If things don't go quite as planned, you have to be able to brush it off, stay focused on the music, and move on. Oddly enough, the number of successes you will have will surprise you if you strike a balance between aspirations and the cold, hard realities of working in showbiz.

Some gigs will be good; others will be a drag. Some shows will be profitable; others will spell a loss. Sometimes you'll have a large, attentive audience; other times you'll have six people dozing off at the bar. Can you laugh it off when things don't go as planned? If so, then you'll enjoy the experience of performing with a band a lot more.

Levels of Musicianship

If you'd like to play music professionally or semiprofessionally, you should get a sense of how the music business works. But first it's important to understand the five basic levels, or ranks, of musicianship. Following is a generalized system of ranking. Bear in mind that some gray areas always exist.

Amateur

Amateur musicians include beginner to intermediate-level players, those who do not get paid to perform, and those who play strictly for fun. Amateurs are often music pupils, and these students can be young or old. There are really two categories for amateurs: the recreational musician and the novice student.

Semiprofessional

Semiprofessionals play for money but do not make a living as a musician. Semiprofessionals are usually college students or adults who work day jobs (or go to school) and gig occasionally at night. Semiprofessionals tend to play low-profile, localized events. Further, they generally receive little compensation.

Journeyman Professional

Journeymen professionals are highly skilled, experienced, and often extremely gifted musicians. They make their living as a musician, though they still work mostly in a localized setting. Most journeymen are freelance players who usually play a wide variety of styles. This chameleon-like quality keeps them in work. Journeymen are sometimes hired to accompany touring celebrities who come through town looking for local players to back them up. Journeymen musicians also tend to be unionized. Subsequently, they are usually called hired guns or mercenaries. Hired guns are musicians who play strictly for money. They do this because music is their profession and often their only source of income.

Distinguished Professional

Distinguished professionals could also be called semicelebrities. These musicians usually have a small- to medium-sized fan base, and younger musicians tend to admire them for their accomplishments. Distinguished professionals almost always have equipment endorsements and are featured in trade magazines, and their resumes boast stints in bands led by major celebrities. Distinguished professionals make a good buck doing what they do. However, on the down side, they often spend most of their careers on the road.

Major Celebrity

This category is fairly self-explanatory. Major celebrities are superstars who play only on an international level, and they are almost always signed to major record labels. This, however, doesn't mean that they are necessary more talented (or more skilled) than journeymen or distinguished professionals. Some celebrities are artistic geniuses; others are just talented entertainers. Often major celebrities are singers, and many of them go on to attain legend status. Celebrity musicians are always well compensated and they have a gigantic fan base. Paul McCartney and Sting are examples of celebrity bassists.

The Music Industry

It's time to take a look at the music industry. If you're a performing musician, it's important to know how each element in the industry functions. Following is a brief description of some key players and movers and shakers in the music industry.

Major Record Labels

Universal Music Group, Sony Music Entertainment, EMI Group, Warner Brothers Music, and BMG Entertainment are collectively known as the Big Five record labels. These are massive, global corporations, and each company has several subsidiaries. Most of the CDs and records you own were probably released by one of these music conglomerates.

Getting signed to a major label is increasingly difficult. However, if your band is selling a lot of CDs, charting in an industry magazine, and playing to large audiences in established clubs, you just might see an A&R (artist & repertoire) representative scouting you out. But beware: always seek the counsel of an entertainment lawyer before signing any contracts with record labels.

Independent Record Labels

Independent record labels are becoming more and more influential since they often break new artists. Some indie labels are becoming so successful they have even become substantial corporations. Despite their independence, major labels still tend to distribute music released by indie labels. For example, Universal Music distributes albums by the well-known jazz label ECM. Nonetheless, indie labels have become a practical solution for musicians looking to break into the scene. More and more musicians are creating their own indie labels too.

Clubs

Clubs give musicians a chance to strut their stuff in front of an audience. You get gigs at clubs by convincing owners, promoters, and/or booking agents that you have some audience draw. Compensation at clubs varies greatly. If you're well established, you can usually ask for monetary guarantees. If you're a newcomer or an unknown artist, you might get paid a percentage of the entrance fee. This is usually called "the door." No matter what the situation, it's very important to promote your event. If you can't put butts in seats, you won't get asked back.

Promoters and Booking Agents

Promoters and booking agents come in all shapes and sizes. Some are aboveboard professionals; others can be shady spin doctors. Both are in the business of making money for themselves, but they do help bands get work and help to spread the word about concerts through their various promotional ideas and schemes. Often, promoters and bookers put together package deals to sell a concert to the public. For example, they might hire three, four, or five bands to play one after another at a given venue. Even if the bands don't have a big draw, the rotating crowds keep the ticket and bar sales up. Festivals work the same way only on a larger scale.

Producers, Managers, and Entertainment Lawyers

In the music business, the word *producer* has a double meaning. It could mean someone who conceives of and organizes concert events (much like a promoter). Music producers can also be studio personnel who are brought in as hired guns to help organize, polish, or revamp a band's sound. Producers help refine, hone, and perfect a group's overall musical approach. In fact, a producer may totally overhaul a band's sound in the studio. Many bands attribute successful records to the insights and vision of a producer.

Managers take on a variety of roles. If you have a good manager, he or she will facilitate just about every aspect of your career from getting you gigs to soliciting record labels to hiring a publicist. In return, managers get a piece of your earnings, whether it's through gigs, CD sales, legal downloads, merchandizing, or all of the above.

Entertainment lawyers help you to understand your rights as a musician. You should never sign a contract without having a lawyer review it first. Contracts contain lots of loopholes and legalese, which can confuse even the most detail-oriented reader. Some lawyers also shop your music to record labels. However, attorneys work less and less on spec (without being paid upfront) anymore, and fees can be high.

The music business is far from fair, and success can be somewhat random. Since the music industry has become a multibillion-dollar business, it has become a tangled web of economic, social, and even political complexities. More and more, the business disregards artistry and artist development in favor of quick moneymakers, one-hit wonders, and fly-by-night trends. However, if you keep your wits about you, make informed decisions, work hard, and maintain a realistic outlook, you will enjoy this business and get something positive out of it.

The Triangle of Success

As you get ready to explore new musical vistas, you should always remember the triangle of success. As you know, a triangle has three angles. In this context, these angles represent:

- Practice
- Performance
- Listening

If you engage in these three activities on a regular basis you will become a formidable musician. In other words, your musical abilities will grow sharper and more acute every day. You've probably heard the axiom that a chain is only as strong as its weakest link. Similarly, the triangle of success is only as strong as its weakest angle. So the goal is to focus on each angle equally. This way you will have all the bases covered. (No pun intended!)

Musicians have long referred to practicing as *woodshedding*. Metaphorically speaking, you must get into the woodshed to hone your skills. Practice has been stressed throughout this book, so it's probably an obvious recommendation by now. However, if you're still unsure about the value of practice remember this: without diligence and hard work, you will never develop the musical vocabulary you need to become a great bass player. Technique can only be learned through practice. Moreover, your creative voice will develop, in part, as a result of practice.

Performance is another critical angle of success. Performing may be the goal of most musicians; however, it's also integral to your education. Only through performance will you understand what you really can play. You might be able to play something in the practice room, but in front of an audience you freeze up or it doesn't come out right. Performing is a kind of rite of passage, and it is the ultimate measure of your skills. Becoming a seasoned performer isn't easy. It's hard to play your best under pressure or in front of a curious audience.

Performing helps you to better gauge your development. The practice room is too predictable and safe to do this honestly, so you must venture out onto the stage to see what you're really made of. If you have a bad performance, avoid negative internal (or external) dialogue. Instead, focus on how you can make improvements. Always use performing as a learning tool, as an opportunity to truly assess your abilities.

What if I get nervous when I play?
The best way to get over nervousness is to simply play a lot in front of others. In time, you will get used to the feeling of being watched and you will feel less self-conscious. If you have unrelenting performance anxiety, you should incorporate relaxation techniques into your playing. You don't have to secretly suffer from stage fright.

Last but not least, listening is a crucial part of playing any instrument. You can't fully learn about music from reading a book just like you can't experience fine wine by thumbing through a buyer's guide. This is why listening is such a critical factor for success. It's also why this publication includes a reference CD.

As a student of music, you should be constantly searching out new and interesting recordings. Start by listening to the so-called legends of music. Don't just listen to bass legends either. Listen to all musicians: drummers, pianists, guitarists, horn players, orchestras, and so on.

In order to complement and accompany other instruments (including voice), you need to understand the sounds and colors other instruments make. If you fill your life with the resonances and textures of music, you will better relate to your instrument and you will better speak the language of music. Through listening, you will hear what possibilities await you. You might also find the inspiration you need to get to that next level.

Appendix A

Key Innovators and Recordings

The following is a list of essential rock, pop, blues, R & B, jazz, fusion, and Latin bassists with one or two of their finer albums. This list is by no means exhaustive. It's best to think of this list as a point of departure. Note: if the bassist is not the leader, the artist or band name will be listed in parenthesis. Also, only electric bass guitarists are listed here, though some of these musicians also play upright bass. Lastly, some of these bassists cross genres, particularly session giants Carol Kaye, Roscoe Beck, Leland Sklar, Chuck Rainey, Duck Dunn, and others.

Rock and Pop

Michael Anthony—*Diver Down* and *1984* (Van Halen)

Jack Bruce—*Disraeli Gears* (Cream) and *More Jack Than God*

Cliff Burton—*Master of Puppets* (Metallica)

Geezer Butler—*Paranoid* (Black Sabbath)

Les Claypool—*Sailing the Seas of Change* (Primus)

Adam Clayton—*The Joshua Tree* and *How to Dismantle an Atomic Bomb* (U2)

Rick Danko—*Music from Big Pink* (The Band)

John Entwistle—*Tommy* and *Who Are You* (The Who)

Flea—*Blood Sugar Sex Magik* and *Californication* (Red Hot Chili Peppers)

Tony Franklin—*Outrider* (Jimmy Page)

Colin Greenwood—*Ok Computer* (Radiohead)

Tom Hamilton—*Toys in the Attic* (Aerosmith)

Steve Harris—*Killers* (Iron Maiden)

Glenn Hughes—*Machine Head* (Deep Purple)

Darryl Jones—*Bring on the Night* (Sting) and *A Bigger Bang* (The Rolling Stones)

John Paul Jones—*Led Zeppelin I* and *Led Zeppelin II* (Led Zeppelin)

Carol Kaye—*Pet Sounds* (The Beach Boys) and *Boots* (Nancy Sinatra)

Lemmy Kilmister—*Ace of Spades* (Motorhead)

Mark King—*World Machine* (Level 42)

Geddy Lee—*2112* and *Vapor Trails* (Rush)

Tony Levin—*Three of a Perfect Pair* (King Crimson) *Us* (Peter Gabriel)

Nick Lowe—*Seconds of Pleasure* (Rockpile) and *The Convincer*

Graham Maby—*Look Sharp!* (Joe Jackson) and *Ophelia* (Natalie Merchant)

Paul McCartney—*Abbey Road* (The Beatles) and *Driving Rain*

Randy Meisner—*Hotel California* (The Eagles)

John Myung—*Six Degrees of Inner Turbulence* (Dream Theatre)

Krist Novoselic—*Nevermind* (Nirvana)

Pino Palladino—*Sowing the Seeds of Love* (Tears for Fears) and *Endless Wire* (The Who)

Noel Redding—*Axis: Bold as Love* (Jimi Hendrix)

Billy Sheehan—*Sink Your Teeth Into That* (Talas) and *Hey Man* (Mr. Big)

Gene Simmons—*Destroyer* (KISS)

Chris Squire—*Fragile* and *90125* (Yes)

Sting—*Ghost in the Machine* (The Police) and *Ten Summoner's Tales*

Bill Wyman—*Aftermath* and *Tattoo You* (The Rolling Stones)

Country and Western

Roscoe Beck (also a noted blues bassist)—*Top of the World Tour: Live* (The Dixie Chicks)

Leland Sklar—*Joshua Judges Ruth* (Lyle Lovett) *Starting Over* (Reba McEntire)

Bee Spears—*Red Headed Stranger* (Willie Nelson)

R & B, Funk, Soul, and Motown

Bootsy Collins—*America Eats Its Young* (Funkadelic) and *Stretchin' Out in Bootsy's Rubber Band* (Bootsy's Rubber Band)

Larry Graham—*One in a Million You* and *Just Be My Lady*

James Jamerson—*Dance Party* (Martha and the Vandellas) *What's Going One* (Marvin Gaye)

Rick James—*Come Get It!* and *Bustin' Out*

Chuck Rainey—*Spanish Harlem* (Aretha Franklin) and *Body Heat* (Quincy Jones)

Latin

Aston "Family Man" Barrett—*Uprising* (Bob Marley & The Wailers) and *Family Man in Dub*

Lincoln Goines—*World on a String* (Dave Valentin)

Robbie Shakespeare—*Friends* and *Mambo Taxi* (Sly and Robbie)

Oscar Stagnaro—*The Caribbean Jazz Project* (The Caribbean Jazz Project)

Bobby Valentin—*Rey Del Bajo*

Blues, Jazz, and Fusion

Jeff Berlin—*Road Games* (Alan Holdsworth) and *In Harmony's Way*

Richard Bona—*Tiki*

Brian Bromberg—*Brian Bromberg* and *Metal*

Stanley Clarke—*Hymn of the Seventh Galaxy* (Return to Forever) and *If This Bass Could Only Talk*

Donald "Duck" Dunn—*Money and Cigarettes* (Eric Clapton) and *Goodbye Newport Blues* (Muddy Waters)

Nathan East—*Journey* (Fourplay)

Mark Egan—*American Garage* (Pat Metheny) *Wouldn't It Be Nice* (Elements)

Jonas Hellborg—*Mahavishnu* (Mahavishnu Orchestra)

Anthony Jackson—*Gaucho* (Steely Dan) and *The Nightfly* (Donald Fagen)

Jerry Jemmott—*Guess Who* (B.B. King) and *Texas Blues* (Lightnin' Hopkins)

Will Lee—*Don't Stop the Music* (The Brecker Brothers) *Reunion* (Gary Burton)

Marcus Miller—*Silver Rain* and *The Sun Don't Lie*

Jaco Pastorius—*Heavy Weather* (Weather Report) and *Jaco Pastorius*

John Patitucci—*Chick Corea Elektric Band* (Chick Corea) and *On the Corner*

Tommy Shannon—*Texas Flood* (Stevie Ray Vaughan and Double Trouble)

Steve Swallow—*Swallow*

Victor Wooten—*Left of Cool* (Bela Fleck and the Flecktones) and *Soul Circus*

Resources

The following is a list of books, Web sites, and films/DVDs that will help you to learn more about bass playing and the musical concepts discussed in this book. Like Appendix A, this list is by no means exhaustive. Hopefully, it will serve as a springboard for your own research.

Publications

Beginning Electric Bass by David Overthrow
Alfred Publishing, 2000

Bass Guitar: Total Scales Techniques and Applications by Mark John Sternal
MJS Music Publications, 2005

101 Bass Tips: Stuff All the Pros Know and Use by Gary Willis
Hal Leonard Corporation, 2002

Complete Book of Bass Chords by Dana Roth
Mel Bay Publications, 1993

Paul McCartney: Playing the Great Beatles Basslines by Tony Bacon and Gareth Morgan
Backbeat Books, 2006

The Latin Bass Book: A Practical Guide by Oscar Stagnaro and Chuck Sher
Sher Music, 2005

Afro Cuban Slap Bass Lines by Oscar Stagnaro
Berklee Press, 2004

Mel Bay's Complete Jazz Bass Book by Earl Gately
Mel Bay, 1999

Electric Bass Composite by Dan Dean (includes books 1, 2, and 3 in one volume)
Hal Leonard, 1996

Motown Bass: A Step-by-Step Breakdown of the Bass Styles and Techniques of Motown
Hal Leonard, 2000

*The R&B Bass Masters: The Way
They Play* by Ed Friedland
Backbeat Books, 2005

Web Sites
✎ *www.basslinks.com*
✎ *www.electricbass.com*
✎ *www.basslessons.com*
✎ *www.studybass.com*
✎ *www.bassmasta.net*
✎ *www.talkbass.com*
✎ *www.bassplayer.com*
✎ *www.bassbooks.com*
✎ *www.paulmccartney.com*
✎ *www.jacopastorius.com*
✎ *www.rockhall.com*
✎ *www.fender.com*
✎ *www.gibson.com*
✎ *www.ernieball.com*
✎ *www.epiphone.com*
✎ *www.warwickbass.com*
✎ *www.peavey.com*
✎ *www.amazon.com*
✎ *www.wikipedia.com*

Film/DVD
Beginning Bass by Tony Saunders
Music Star Productions, 2005

*The Rock House Method: Learn Rock
Bass* (beginner and intermediate levels available) by Rock House
Rock House, 2005

*Best of Lennon & McCartney for
Bass Guitar* by Bob Efford
Hal Leonard, 2002

Slap Bass: The Ultimate Guide by Ed Friedland
Hal Leonard, 2003

Flea: Adventures in Spontaneous Jamming & Techniques by Flea
Hal Leonard, 2002

Jaco Pastorius: Live and Outrageous by Jaco Pastorius
Shanachie, 2007

The Space Within Us by Paul McCartney
A&E Home Video, 2006

*Victor Wooten Live at Bass Day
'98* by Victor Wooten
Hal Leonard, 2001

Index

A

Accelerando, defined, 208

Accents, 208

Accessories. *See* Tools and accessories

Adagio, defined, 207

Afro-Cuban grooves, 124–27, 171–72

Agents and promoters, 258–59

Allegro, defined, 207

Alternate tunings, 90–91

Amplifiers

    buying (types and considerations), 4–5

    connecting and turning on, 21–22

    maintenance, 9–10

Anatomy of electric bass, 12–13

Andante, defined, 207

Arpeggios, 58, 61, 66, 90, 101–2, 127–28, 149, 154–55, 219, 236–37

A tempo, defined, 208

B

Band-in-a-Box, 200–201

Bands, 254–56

Bass clef, 24–26

Bass line, 73–74

Beat, playing behind, middle, ahead of, 77–79

Bird's eye (fermata), 208

Blues and jazz, 93–106, 264

    creating bass lines, 190–94

    down-home blues lines, 152–54

    harmonics for, 104–5, 106, 176, 177–78

    history of, 94–95

    integrating scales, 144–45

    Jaco Pastorius and, 95, 96, 104, 160, 175

    ostinatos, 76, 104, 106, 115, 158

    pedal tones, 104

    scales, 140–45

    shuffle (swing), 97–99

    snaky jazz licks, 160–61

    soloing in blues and rock, 139–46

    soloing in jazz, 146–50

    two-beat bass lines, 99–100

    walking bass lines, 101–4

"Blues for Willie Dixon," 167–69

Brazilian bass lines, 122–24

Buying equipment

    accessories, 5–8

    amplifiers, 4–5

    color and style, 2–4

    effects, 7–8

    investment amount, 2

    right fit, 2–4

C

Calypso and soca, 121, 130–31

Cases, 8

Charts. *See* Reading charts and lead sheets

Chord extensions, 87–90. *See also* Extended harmonies

YOU SHOULD CAREFULLY READ THE FOLLOWING TERMS AND CONDITIONS BEFORE USING THIS SOFTWARE PRODUCT. INSTALLING AND USING THIS PRODUCT INDICATES YOUR ACCEPTANCE OF THESE CONDITIONS. IF YOU DO NOT AGREE WITH THESE TERMS AND CONDITIONS, DO NOT INSTALL THE SOFTWARE AND RETURN THIS PACKAGE PROMPTLY FOR A FULL REFUND.

1. Grant of License

This software package is protected under United States copyright law and international treaty. You are hereby entitled to one copy of the enclosed software and are allowed by law to make one backup copy or to copy the contents of the disks onto a single hard disk and keep the originals as your backup or archival copy. United States copyright law prohibits you from making a copy of this software for use on any computer other than your own computer. United States copyright law also prohibits you from copying any written material included in this software package without first obtaining the permission of F+W Publications, Inc.

2. Restrictions

You, the end-user, are hereby prohibited from the following:
You may not rent or lease the Software or make copies to rent or lease for profit or for any other purpose.
You may not disassemble or reverse compile for the purposes of reverse engineering the Software.
You may not modify or adapt the Software or documentation in whole or in part, including, but not limited to, translating or creating derivative works.

3. Transfer

You may transfer the Software to another person, provided that (a) you transfer all of the Software and documentation to the same transferee; (b) you do not retain any copies; and (c) the transferee is informed of and agrees to the terms and conditions of this Agreement.

4. Termination

This Agreement and your license to use the Software can be terminated without notice if you fail to comply with any of the provisions set forth in this Agreement. Upon termination of this Agreement, you promise to destroy all copies of the software including backup or archival copies as well as any documentation associated with the Software. All disclaimers of warranties and limitation of liability set forth in this Agreement shall survive any termination of this Agreement.

5. Limited Warranty

F+W Publications, Inc. warrants that the Software will perform according to the manual and other written materials accompanying the Software for a period of 30 days from the date of receipt. F+W Publications, Inc. does not accept responsibility for any malfunctioning computer hardware or any incompatibilities with existing or new computer hardware technology.

6. Customer Remedies

F+W Publications, Inc.'s entire liability and your exclusive remedy shall be, at the option of F+W Publications, Inc., either refund of your purchase price or repair and/or replacement of Software that does not meet this Limited Warranty. Proof of purchase shall be required. This Limited Warranty will be voided if Software failure was caused by abuse, neglect, accident or misapplication. All replacement Software will be warranted based on the remainder of the warranty or the full 30 days, whichever is shorter and will be subject to the terms of the Agreement.

7. No Other Warranties

F+W PUBLICATIONS, INC., TO THE FULLEST EXTENT OF THE LAW, DISCLAIMS ALL OTHER WARRANTIES, OTHER THAN THE LIMITED WARRANTY IN PARAGRAPH 5, EITHER EXPRESS OR IMPLIED, ASSOCIATED WITH ITS SOFTWARE, INCLUDING BUT NOT LIMITED TO IMPLIED WARRANTIES OF MERCHANTABILITY AND FITNESS FOR A PARTICULAR PURPOSE, WITH REGARD TO THE SOFTWARE AND ITS ACCOMPANYING WRITTEN MATERIALS. THIS LIMITED WARRANTY GIVES YOU SPECIFIC LEGAL RIGHTS. DEPENDING UPON WHERE THIS SOFTWARE WAS PURCHASED, YOU MAY HAVE OTHER RIGHTS.

8. Limitations on Remedies

TO THE MAXIMUM EXTENT PERMITTED BY LAW, F+W PUBLICATIONS, INC. SHALL NOT BE HELD LIABLE FOR ANY DAMAGES WHATSOEVER, INCLUDING WITHOUT LIMITATION, ANY LOSS FROM PERSONAL INJURY, LOSS OF BUSINESS PROFITS, BUSINESS INTERRUPTION, BUSINESS INFORMATION OR ANY OTHER PECUNIARY LOSS ARISING OUT OF THE USE OF THIS SOFTWARE.
This applies even if F+W Publications, Inc. has been advised of the possibility of such damages. F+W Publications, Inc.'s entire liability under any provision of this agreement shall be limited to the amount actually paid by you for the Software. Because some states may not allow for this type of limitation of liability, the above limitation may not apply to you.
THE WARRANTY AND REMEDIES SET FORTH ABOVE ARE EXCLUSIVE AND IN LIEU OF ALL OTHERS, ORAL OR WRITTEN, EXPRESS OR IMPLIED. No F+W Publications, Inc. dealer, distributor, agent, or employee is authorized to make any modification or addition to the warranty.

9. General

This Agreement shall be governed by the laws of the United States of America and the Commonwealth of Massachusetts. If you have any questions concerning this Agreement, contact F+W Publications, Inc., via Adams Media at 508-427-7100. Or write to us at: Adams Media, an F+W Publications Company, 57 Littlefield Street, Avon, MA 02322.

THE EVERYTHING SERIES!

BUSINESS & PERSONAL FINANCE

Everything® Accounting Book
Everything® Budgeting Book, 2nd Ed.
Everything® Business Planning Book
Everything® Coaching and Mentoring Book, 2nd Ed.
Everything® Fundraising Book
Everything® Get Out of Debt Book
Everything® Grant Writing Book, 2nd Ed.
Everything® Guide to Buying Foreclosures
Everything® Guide to Mortgages
Everything® Guide to Personal Finance for Single Mothers
Everything® Home-Based Business Book, 2nd Ed.
Everything® Homebuying Book, 2nd Ed.
Everything® Homeselling Book, 2nd Ed.
Everything® Human Resource Management Book
Everything® Improve Your Credit Book
Everything® Investing Book, 2nd Ed.
Everything® Landlording Book
Everything® Leadership Book, 2nd Ed.
Everything® Managing People Book, 2nd Ed.
Everything® Negotiating Book
Everything® Online Auctions Book
Everything® Online Business Book
Everything® Personal Finance Book
Everything® Personal Finance in Your 20s & 30s Book, 2nd Ed.
Everything® Project Management Book, 2nd Ed.
Everything® Real Estate Investing Book
Everything® Retirement Planning Book
Everything® Robert's Rules Book, $7.95
Everything® Selling Book
Everything® Start Your Own Business Book, 2nd Ed.
Everything® Wills & Estate Planning Book

COOKING

Everything® Barbecue Cookbook
Everything® Bartender's Book, 2nd Ed., $9.95
Everything® Calorie Counting Cookbook
Everything® Cheese Book
Everything® Chinese Cookbook
Everything® Classic Recipes Book
Everything® Cocktail Parties & Drinks Book
Everything® College Cookbook
Everything® Cooking for Baby and Toddler Book
Everything® Cooking for Two Cookbook
Everything® Diabetes Cookbook
Everything® Easy Gourmet Cookbook
Everything® Fondue Cookbook
Everything® Fondue Party Book
Everything® Gluten-Free Cookbook
Everything® Glycemic Index Cookbook
Everything® Grilling Cookbook
Everything® Healthy Meals in Minutes Cookbook
Everything® Holiday Cookbook
Everything® Indian Cookbook
Everything® Italian Cookbook

Everything® Lactose-Free Cookbook
Everything® Low-Carb Cookbook
Everything® Low-Cholesterol Cookbook
Everything® Low-Fat High-Flavor Cookbook
Everything® Low-Salt Cookbook
Everything® Meals for a Month Cookbook
Everything® Meals on a Budget Cookbook
Everything® Mediterranean Cookbook
Everything® Mexican Cookbook
Everything® No Trans Fat Cookbook
Everything® One-Pot Cookbook
Everything® Pizza Cookbook
Everything® Quick and Easy 30-Minute,
    5-Ingredient Cookbook
Everything® Quick Meals Cookbook
Everything® Slow Cooker Cookbook
Everything® Slow Cooking for a Crowd Cookbook
Everything® Soup Cookbook
Everything® Stir-Fry Cookbook
Everything® Sugar-Free Cookbook
Everything® Tapas and Small Plates Cookbook
Everything® Tex-Mex Cookbook
Everything® Thai Cookbook
Everything® Vegetarian Cookbook
Everything® Whole-Grain, High-Fiber Cookbook
Everything® Wild Game Cookbook
Everything® Wine Book, 2nd Ed.

GAMES

Everything® 15-Minute Sudoku Book, $9.95
Everything® 30-Minute Sudoku Book, $9.95
Everything® Bible Crosswords Book, $9.95
Everything® Blackjack Strategy Book
Everything® Brain Strain Book, $9.95
Everything® Bridge Book
Everything® Card Games Book
Everything® Card Tricks Book, $9.95
Everything® Casino Gambling Book, 2nd Ed.
Everything® Chess Basics Book
Everything® Craps Strategy Book
Everything® Crossword and Puzzle Book
Everything® Crossword Challenge Book
Everything® Crosswords for the Beach Book, $9.95
Everything® Cryptic Crosswords Book, $9.95
Everything® Cryptograms Book, $9.95
Everything® Easy Crosswords Book
Everything® Easy Kakuro Book, $9.95
Everything® Easy Large-Print Crosswords Book
Everything® Games Book, 2nd Ed.
Everything® Giant Sudoku Book, $9.95
Everything® Giant Word Search Book
Everything® Kakuro Challenge Book, $9.95
Everything® Large-Print Crossword Challenge Book
Everything® Large-Print Crosswords Book
Everything® Lateral Thinking Puzzles Book, $9.95
Everything® Literary Crosswords Book, $9.95
Everything® Mazes Book
Everything® Memory Booster Puzzles Book, $9.95
Everything® Movie Crosswords Book, $9.95

Everything® Music Crosswords Book, $9.95
Everything® Online Poker Book
Everything® Pencil Puzzles Book, $9.95
Everything® Poker Strategy Book
Everything® Pool & Billiards Book
Everything® Puzzles for Commuters Book, $9.95
Everything® Puzzles for Dog Lovers Book, $9.95
Everything® Sports Crosswords Book, $9.95
Everything® Test Your IQ Book, $9.95
Everything® Texas Hold 'Em Book, $9.95
Everything® Travel Crosswords Book, $9.95
Everything® TV Crosswords Book, $9.95
Everything® Word Games Challenge Book
Everything® Word Scramble Book
Everything® Word Search Book

HEALTH

Everything® Alzheimer's Book
Everything® Diabetes Book
Everything® First Aid Book, $9.95
Everything® Health Guide to Adult Bipolar Disorder
Everything® Health Guide to Arthritis
Everything® Health Guide to Controlling Anxiety
Everything® Health Guide to Depression
Everything® Health Guide to Fibromyalgia
Everything® Health Guide to Menopause, 2nd Ed.
Everything® Health Guide to Migraines
Everything® Health Guide to OCD
Everything® Health Guide to PMS
Everything® Health Guide to Postpartum Care
Everything® Health Guide to Thyroid Disease
Everything® Hypnosis Book
Everything® Low Cholesterol Book
Everything® Menopause Book
Everything® Nutrition Book
Everything® Reflexology Book
Everything® Stress Management Book

HISTORY

Everything® American Government Book
Everything® American History Book, 2nd Ed.
Everything® Civil War Book
Everything® Freemasons Book
Everything® Irish History & Heritage Book
Everything® Middle East Book
Everything® World War II Book, 2nd Ed.

HOBBIES

Everything® Candlemaking Book
Everything® Cartooning Book
Everything® Coin Collecting Book
Everything® Digital Photography Book, 2nd Ed.
Everything® Drawing Book
Everything® Family Tree Book, 2nd Ed.
Everything® Knitting Book
Everything® Knots Book
Everything® Photography Book
Everything® Quilting Book

Everything® Sewing Book
Everything® Soapmaking Book, 2nd Ed.
Everything® Woodworking Book

HOME IMPROVEMENT

Everything® Feng Shui Book
Everything® Feng Shui Decluttering Book, $9.95
Everything® Fix-It Book
Everything® Green Living Book
Everything® Home Decorating Book
Everything® Home Storage Solutions Book
Everything® Homebuilding Book
Everything® Organize Your Home Book, 2nd Ed.

KIDS' BOOKS

All titles are $7.95
Everything® Fairy Tales Book, $14.95
Everything® Kids' Animal Puzzle & Activity Book
Everything® Kids' Astronomy Book
Everything® Kids' Baseball Book, 5th Ed.
Everything® Kids' Bible Trivia Book
Everything® Kids' Bugs Book
Everything® Kids' Cars and Trucks Puzzle and Activity Book
Everything® Kids' Christmas Puzzle & Activity Book
**Everything® Kids' Connect the Dots
Puzzle and Activity Book**
Everything® Kids' Cookbook
Everything® Kids' Crazy Puzzles Book
Everything® Kids' Dinosaurs Book
Everything® Kids' Environment Book
Everything® Kids' Fairies Puzzle and Activity Book
Everything® Kids' First Spanish Puzzle and Activity Book
Everything® Kids' Football Book
Everything® Kids' Gross Cookbook
Everything® Kids' Gross Hidden Pictures Book
Everything® Kids' Gross Jokes Book
Everything® Kids' Gross Mazes Book
Everything® Kids' Gross Puzzle & Activity Book
Everything® Kids' Halloween Puzzle & Activity Book
Everything® Kids' Hidden Pictures Book
Everything® Kids' Horses Book
Everything® Kids' Joke Book
Everything® Kids' Knock Knock Book
Everything® Kids' Learning French Book
Everything® Kids' Learning Spanish Book
Everything® Kids' Magical Science Experiments Book
Everything® Kids' Math Puzzles Book
Everything® Kids' Mazes Book
Everything® Kids' Money Book
Everything® Kids' Nature Book
Everything® Kids' Pirates Puzzle and Activity Book
Everything® Kids' Presidents Book
Everything® Kids' Princess Puzzle and Activity Book
Everything® Kids' Puzzle Book
Everything® Kids' Racecars Puzzle and Activity Book
Everything® Kids' Riddles & Brain Teasers Book
Everything® Kids' Science Experiments Book
Everything® Kids' Sharks Book
Everything® Kids' Soccer Book
Everything® Kids' Spies Puzzle and Activity Book
Everything® Kids' States Book
Everything® Kids' Travel Activity Book
Everything® Kids' Word Search Puzzle and Activity Book

LANGUAGE

Everything® Conversational Japanese Book with CD, $19.95
Everything® French Grammar Book
Everything® French Phrase Book, $9.95
Everything® French Verb Book, $9.95
Everything® German Practice Book with CD, $19.95
Everything® Inglés Book
Everything® Intermediate Spanish Book with CD, $19.95
Everything® Italian Practice Book with CD, $19.95
Everything® Learning Brazilian Portuguese Book with CD, $19.95
Everything® Learning French Book with CD, 2nd Ed., $19.95
Everything® Learning German Book
Everything® Learning Italian Book
Everything® Learning Latin Book
Everything® Learning Russian Book with CD, $19.95
Everything® Learning Spanish Book
Everything® Learning Spanish Book with CD, 2nd Ed., $19.95
Everything® Russian Practice Book with CD, $19.95
Everything® Sign Language Book
Everything® Spanish Grammar Book
Everything® Spanish Phrase Book, $9.95
Everything® Spanish Practice Book with CD, $19.95
Everything® Spanish Verb Book, $9.95
Everything® Speaking Mandarin Chinese Book with CD, $19.95

MUSIC

Everything® Bass Guitar Book with CD, $19.95
Everything® Drums Book with CD, $19.95
Everything® Guitar Book with CD, 2nd Ed., $19.95
Everything® Guitar Chords Book with CD, $19.95
Everything® Harmonica Book with CD, $15.95
Everything® Home Recording Book
Everything® Music Theory Book with CD, $19.95
Everything® Reading Music Book with CD, $19.95
Everything® Rock & Blues Guitar Book with CD, $19.95
Everything® Rock & Blues Piano Book with CD, $19.95
Everything® Songwriting Book

NEW AGE

Everything® Astrology Book, 2nd Ed.
Everything® Birthday Personology Book
Everything® Dreams Book, 2nd Ed.
Everything® Love Signs Book, $9.95
Everything® Love Spells Book, $9.95
Everything® Paganism Book
Everything® Palmistry Book
Everything® Psychic Book
Everything® Reiki Book
Everything® Sex Signs Book, $9.95
Everything® Spells & Charms Book, 2nd Ed.
Everything® Tarot Book, 2nd Ed.
Everything® Toltec Wisdom Book
Everything® Wicca & Witchcraft Book, 2nd Ed.

PARENTING

Everything® Baby Names Book, 2nd Ed.
Everything® Baby Shower Book, 2nd Ed.
Everything® Baby Sign Language Book with DVD
Everything® Baby's First Year Book
Everything® Birthing Book

Everything® Breastfeeding Book
Everything® Father-to-Be Book
Everything® Father's First Year Book
Everything® Get Ready for Baby Book, 2nd Ed.
Everything® Get Your Baby to Sleep Book, $9.95
Everything® Getting Pregnant Book
Everything® Guide to Pregnancy Over 35
Everything® Guide to Raising a One-Year-Old
Everything® Guide to Raising a Two-Year-Old
Everything® Guide to Raising Adolescent Boys
Everything® Guide to Raising Adolescent Girls
Everything® Mother's First Year Book
Everything® Parent's Guide to Childhood Illnesses
Everything® Parent's Guide to Children and Divorce
Everything® Parent's Guide to Children with ADD/ADHD
Everything® Parent's Guide to Children with Asperger's Syndrome
Everything® Parent's Guide to Children with Asthma
Everything® Parent's Guide to Children with Autism
Everything® Parent's Guide to Children with Bipolar Disorder
Everything® Parent's Guide to Children with Depression
Everything® Parent's Guide to Children with Dyslexia
Everything® Parent's Guide to Children with Juvenile Diabetes
Everything® Parent's Guide to Positive Discipline
Everything® Parent's Guide to Raising a Successful Child
Everything® Parent's Guide to Raising Boys
Everything® Parent's Guide to Raising Girls
Everything® Parent's Guide to Raising Siblings
Everything® Parent's Guide to Sensory Integration Disorder
Everything® Parent's Guide to Tantrums
Everything® Parent's Guide to the Strong-Willed Child
Everything® Parenting a Teenager Book
Everything® Potty Training Book, $9.95
Everything® Pregnancy Book, 3rd Ed.
Everything® Pregnancy Fitness Book
Everything® Pregnancy Nutrition Book
Everything® Pregnancy Organizer, 2nd Ed., $16.95
Everything® Toddler Activities Book
Everything® Toddler Book
Everything® Tween Book
Everything® Twins, Triplets, and More Book

PETS

Everything® Aquarium Book
Everything® Boxer Book
Everything® Cat Book, 2nd Ed.
Everything® Chihuahua Book
Everything® Cooking for Dogs Book
Everything® Dachshund Book
Everything® Dog Book, 2nd Ed.
Everything® Dog Grooming Book
Everything® Dog Health Book
Everything® Dog Obedience Book
Everything® Dog Owner's Organizer, $16.95
Everything® Dog Training and Tricks Book
Everything® German Shepherd Book
Everything® Golden Retriever Book
Everything® Horse Book
Everything® Horse Care Book
Everything® Horseback Riding Book
Everything® Labrador Retriever Book
Everything® Poodle Book
Everything® Pug Book

Everything® Puppy Book
Everything® Rottweiler Book
Everything® Small Dogs Book
Everything® Tropical Fish Book
Everything® Yorkshire Terrier Book

REFERENCE

Everything® American Presidents Book
Everything® Blogging Book
Everything® Build Your Vocabulary Book, $9.95
Everything® Car Care Book
Everything® Classical Mythology Book
Everything® Da Vinci Book
Everything® Divorce Book
Everything® Einstein Book
Everything® Enneagram Book
Everything® Etiquette Book, 2nd Ed.
Everything® Guide to C. S. Lewis & Narnia
Everything® Guide to Edgar Allan Poe
Everything® Guide to Understanding Philosophy
Everything® Inventions and Patents Book
Everything® Jacqueline Kennedy Onassis Book
Everything® John F. Kennedy Book
Everything® Mafia Book
Everything® Martin Luther King Jr. Book
Everything® Philosophy Book
Everything® Pirates Book
Everything® Private Investigation Book
Everything® Psychology Book
Everything® Public Speaking Book, $9.95
Everything® Shakespeare Book, 2nd Ed.

RELIGION

Everything® Angels Book
Everything® Bible Book
Everything® Bible Study Book with CD, $19.95
Everything® Buddhism Book
Everything® Catholicism Book
Everything® Christianity Book
Everything® Gnostic Gospels Book
Everything® History of the Bible Book
Everything® Jesus Book
Everything® Jewish History & Heritage Book
Everything® Judaism Book
Everything® Kabbalah Book
Everything® Koran Book
Everything® Mary Book
Everything® Mary Magdalene Book
Everything® Prayer Book
Everything® Saints Book, 2nd Ed.
Everything® Torah Book
Everything® Understanding Islam Book
Everything® Women of the Bible Book
Everything® World's Religions Book

SCHOOL & CAREERS

Everything® Career Tests Book
Everything® College Major Test Book
Everything® College Survival Book, 2nd Ed.
Everything® Cover Letter Book, 2nd Ed.
Everything® Filmmaking Book
Everything® Get-a-Job Book, 2nd Ed.
Everything® Guide to Being a Paralegal
Everything® Guide to Being a Personal Trainer
Everything® Guide to Being a Real Estate Agent
Everything® Guide to Being a Sales Rep
Everything® Guide to Being an Event Planner
Everything® Guide to Careers in Health Care
Everything® Guide to Careers in Law Enforcement
Everything® Guide to Government Jobs
Everything® Guide to Starting and Running a Catering Business
Everything® Guide to Starting and Running a Restaurant
Everything® Job Interview Book, 2nd Ed.
Everything® New Nurse Book
Everything® New Teacher Book
Everything® Paying for College Book
Everything® Practice Interview Book
Everything® Resume Book, 3rd Ed.
Everything® Study Book

SELF-HELP

Everything® Body Language Book
Everything® Dating Book, 2nd Ed.
Everything® Great Sex Book
Everything® Self-Esteem Book
Everything® Tantric Sex Book

SPORTS & FITNESS

Everything® Easy Fitness Book
Everything® Fishing Book
Everything® Krav Maga for Fitness Book
Everything® Running Book, 2nd Ed.

TRAVEL

Everything® Family Guide to Coastal Florida
Everything® Family Guide to Cruise Vacations
Everything® Family Guide to Hawaii
Everything® Family Guide to Las Vegas, 2nd Ed.
Everything® Family Guide to Mexico
Everything® Family Guide to New England, 2nd Ed.
Everything® Family Guide to New York City, 3rd Ed.
Everything® Family Guide to RV Travel & Campgrounds
Everything® Family Guide to the Caribbean
Everything® Family Guide to the Disneyland® Resort, California Adventure®, Universal Studios®, and the Anaheim Area, 2nd Ed.
Everything® Family Guide to the Walt Disney World Resort®, Universal Studios®, and Greater Orlando, 5th Ed.
Everything® Family Guide to Timeshares
Everything® Family Guide to Washington D.C., 2nd Ed.

WEDDINGS

Everything® Bachelorette Party Book, $9.95
Everything® Bridesmaid Book, $9.95
Everything® Destination Wedding Book
Everything® Father of the Bride Book, $9.95
Everything® Groom Book, $9.95
Everything® Mother of the Bride Book, $9.95
Everything® Outdoor Wedding Book
Everything® Wedding Book, 3rd Ed.
Everything® Wedding Checklist, $9.95
Everything® Wedding Etiquette Book, $9.95
Everything® Wedding Organizer, 2nd Ed., $16.95
Everything® Wedding Shower Book, $9.95
Everything® Wedding Vows Book, $9.95
Everything® Wedding Workout Book
Everything® Weddings on a Budget Book, 2nd Ed., $9.95

WRITING

Everything® Creative Writing Book
Everything® Get Published Book, 2nd Ed.
Everything® Grammar and Style Book, 2nd Ed.
Everything® Guide to Magazine Writing
Everything® Guide to Writing a Book Proposal
Everything® Guide to Writing a Novel
Everything® Guide to Writing Children's Books
Everything® Guide to Writing Copy
Everything® Guide to Writing Graphic Novels
Everything® Guide to Writing Research Papers
Everything® Improve Your Writing Book, 2nd Ed.
Everything® Writing Poetry Book